TO GOD BE THE GLORY

The Revelation of Jesus Christ
Chapters 2 and 3

HEAR WHAT
THE SPIRIT SAYS
TO THE CHURCHES

by Marjorie Merz Fennell

Hear What the Spirit Says to the Churches
Copyright © 2022 by Marjorie Merz Fennell

All rights reserved. In order to prevent misuse, no part of this publication may be reproduced or translated or transmitted in any form or by any means, electronic or mechanical, including photocopy, recording, or any information storage or retrieval system without express written permission from the copyright owner.

For further details and/or permission, please contact Dale Dickson joyinservingjc@gmail.com

Unless otherwise noted, all Scripture quotations are taken from the New American Standard Bible® (NASB), Copyright © 1960, 1962, 1963, 1968, 1971, 1972, 1973, 1975, 1977, 1995 by The Lockman Foundation. Used by permission. www.Lockman.org

Note the following Bible version abbreviations:
AMP—The Amplified Bible
KJV—King James Version
NIV—New International Version
Wuest—The New Testament: An Expanded Translation

First Edition: 2022
Hear What the Spirit Says to the Churches / Marjorie Merz Fennell
Paperback ISBN: 978-1-951304-86-7
eBook ISBN: 978-1-951304-87-4

It was He [Christ] who gave some to be apostles, some to be prophets, some to be evangelists, and some to be pastors and teachers, to prepare God's people for works of service, so that the body of Christ may be built up until we all reach unity in the faith and in the knowledge of the Son of God and become mature, attaining to the whole measure of the fullness of Christ.

Then we will no longer be infants, tossed back and forth by the waves, and blown here and there by every wind of teaching and by the cunning and craftiness of men in their deceitful scheming. Instead, speaking the truth in love, we will in all things grow up into Him who is the Head, that is, Christ. From Him the whole body, joined and held together by every supporting ligament, grows and builds itself up in love, as each part does its work.

Ephesians 4:11-16 NIV

Table of Contents

Foreword _____ 1
The Backdrop _____ 5
Chapter One: Something Is Missing _____ 10
Chapter Two: In The Face of Persecution _____ 19
Chapter Three: Stop Being Silent _____ 24
Chapter Four: Deal with Jezebel _____ 29
Chapter Five: On The Verge of Shipwreck _____ 37
Chapter Six: Deep Calls to Deep _____ 43
Chapter Seven: Behold the Cliff _____ 50
Chapter Eight: A Trumpet Call _____ 61
Chapter Nine: A Deeper Reflection in Truth _____ 71
Chapter Ten: The Judgment of Believers _____ 74
Chapter Eleven: The Glorified One _____ 76
Chapter Twelve: A Revived Church _____ 81
References _____ 89
About the Author _____ 90

Foreword

It was in the first discussion time of Kay Arthur's Precept upon Precept Study on Revelation in September 2012 that the Holy Spirit began illuminating it to me in a personal way; much like the glorified Christ also did for the readers and hearers of His seven messages to the churches as they were being read. It was as though He were standing right there in front of them. That is how He also encountered John on the island of Patmos when he fell like a dead man at His feet, having just seen Him in spirit. And as the glorified Christ laid His hand upon him, He said: *"Don't be afraid…"* For this is how God has always intended to speak to us in Christ Jesus: in the glory of His presence face to face…and especially in specific seasons and at appointed times in our walk with Him. Having been imprisoned on the isle of Patmos for his faith in Jesus Christ, John was His chosen recipient for the revelation during a very trying time in his life here on earth. It was also in the midst of Job's fiery ordeal that he too was brought to understand his God in a fresh new way. And as the Holy Spirit led me through a study of the first three chapters of this prophetic book (and thus a book of both promises and warnings), I found Job's response to be mine: *I have heard of You by the hearing of the ear; but now my eye sees You; therefore, I retract, and repent in dust and ashes.* Job 42:6

When the study group broke for the summer in 2013, I desired to go deeper into the seven messages in Chapters 2 and 3. And as I did, I began to write what was unfolding before me. As I reflected on each one and wrote what was given to me, it became like a grand orchestra made up of various instruments—each one having a part unique to their own design, yet all coming together into one resounding sound! You could even say like a trumpet call: *Behold, the LORD GOD will come with might, with His arm ruling for Him. Behold, His reward is with Him and His recompense before Him.* Isaiah 40:10

What you are about to read is not an expository commentary, yet I believe it will still bring out tones and pitches that you may not have heard before and lend light to the whole. Being more of a prophetic utterance, it's not intended to be a casual or easy or quick read, and it cannot be approached as an exercise of your intellect. It requires a prayerful approach and reflective thought as the Holy Spirit engages you in the reading of it. You may even need to sit with a sentence or two as you wrestle with it, allowing Him to open it up to you. That is why you will see a series of three dots…at times to slow you down in your reading so you are not rushing ahead to the next thought without having grasped the first one or the one following on its heel. And since it is the Spirit who searches the deep things of God for you through His eternal Word, you will want to set aside time to contemplate the mentioned scripture references so you may come into the fullness of each message. Be aware, too, that as you are making your way through each of these messages, they overlap from one message to the next one, like breakers do as they come up on the seashore, or like a mother who tells her child: "I'm going to tell you, and then tell you again, and then tell you what I already told you."

C.H. Spurgeon's words come into play here:

> "Heart-rending is divinely worked and solemnly felt. It is a secret grief that is personally experienced, not in mere form, but as a deep, soul-moving work of the Holy Spirit upon the inmost heart of each believer. It is not

> a matter to be merely talked about and believed in, but keenly and sensitively felt in every living child of the living God. It is powerfully humiliating and completely sin-purging, but it is also preparation for the gracious consolations that proud, unhumbled spirits are unable to receive; and it is distinctly discriminating, for it belongs to the elect of God, and to them alone." (Spurgeon, Morning and Evening, March 2008, p. 706)

One last note: if you are in the five-fold ministry, an elder in a church, or are in ministry or have been called to ministry, whether in a local church or outside it; or if you have received a call from God to ministry and are actively preparing for it or are contemplating such a call - take special note. Beware of the foolish pride that thinks or says to itself either before reading or even during reading that the five messages with correction don't apply to you or that it could never happen to you. Instead, let God do the examination of your heart and let Him be your judge (Hebrews 4:12-13; Jeremiah 17:9-10; 32: 32-34).

In training His children, the heavenly Father is working towards them having a proper mindset…one like His that is pure and heavenly and eternal. How challenging that can be for us! Listen to how it can happen from this scripture: *Coastlands, listen to Me in silence, and let the people gain new strength; let them come forward, then let them speak; let us come together for judgment.* Isaiah 41:1

That is what this book is about: positioning yourself in humbleness of mind to hear what the Spirit is saying, and through a new mindset gain new strength to move forward into your walk and ministry with the Lord. Doing what this scripture says facilitates the posture of a humble and receiving heart with a hearing ear that says, "Yes, Lord, I hear what You are saying." For in these seven messages are a complete and full message in which nothing is lacking—one unified message to all the elect in Christ: the general assembly of God, the mystical body of Jesus Christ, the Bride of Christ.

Let's begin.

THE BACKDROP

Some 60-90 years after the Lord Jesus' bodily resurrection and His ascension into heaven forty days later, God His Father, who sits upon His throne in heaven, had something to say to the Church on earth. One might wonder why. What had happened to her and what was on the horizon that so moved His heart to give this revelation to His Son to impart to His bondservants...His godly ones who had made a covenant with Him by sacrifice? (Psalm 50:3-5).

The urgency for this revelation and the seven messages is discovered in part in the Lord's words in Chapter 1:19c...*and the things which shall be hereafter* (KJV). There's such a sound of finality in His words, isn't there? It's something that's certain to happen, but when you listen more closely, you may hear its swiftness as well...just like when a guillotine blade is released from its ropes and pulleys. As sobering as that is, there is still another urgency in these messages being written and sent to these seven churches. As you will soon see, the Church is floundering at this very critical point in time before the Lord's return. Throughout Chapters 2 and 3, you'll see the monumental struggle she has had in remaining true to her profession of faith in Christ alone without any compromise of any kind. And with a deeper look there, you'll begin to understand that her greatest need is for transformation...not renewal (Romans 12:1-2; 13:11-14).

The Lord Jesus Himself, the One who died and rose again on His Bride's behalf, instructed His apostles shortly before His crucifixion with these timely words: *If anyone would serve Me, he must continue to follow Me – to cleave steadfastly to Me, conform wholly to My example, in living and if need be in dying – and wherever I am, there will My servant be also. If anyone serves Me, the Father will honor him.* John 12:26 AMP

Did you hear within these words what true commitment and heartfelt service looks like for His true disciples…and the intimacy and marks of honor it will bring them into? Did you also hear how the Father's heart beats for such intimacy with His children? He yearns that each one grows up in their union with His Son and into Christ-likeness: that they continue advancing in truth, humbleness of mind, faith, love, and the revelation of Him in His ascension to glory in heaven. It's with their highest good in mind that their heavenly Father urges them on to lay hold of that for which they have already been apprehended by His Son Jesus Christ. For being the wise Father that He is, He knows that only as they persevere in the doing of this will they not be so easily shaken from their true spiritual foundation in His eternal Son; and will then realize experientially their true calling and purpose in the days before them while they are on earth!

You might be wondering what that might be. Jesus alluded to it in one of His parables. Shortly before His triumphal entry into Jerusalem, He said to His disciples who had their hopes up that the kingdom of God was at hand, meaning the Lord's Kingdom reign was going to happen right then and there. He said, therefore, *A certain nobleman went into a far country to receive for himself a kingdom, and to return. And he called his ten servants, and delivered them ten pounds, and said unto them, Occupy till I come.* Luke 19:11-13 KJV

It's also important to understand before you start reading this book that the Greek word *angelos* is read as *angel* in our English translation of the Scriptures. The Greek word means *messenger*.

Whether angelic or human, a messenger in the Bible is always a sent one: one sent with a commission from God…or you could say, sent with His official authoritative sending. One of the first challenges in reading The Revelation of Jesus Christ is to know whether the English word *angel* in Chapters 2 and 3 refers to a heavenly being or a human being. Whenever you are searching for the meaning of a scripture or even a word within a scripture, you must have the immediate context as well as the whole counsel of God in mind from His written Word. Throughout the Bible, in both the Old and New Testaments, you never see a man writing to an angel with a message from God. Never. Always, it is a heavenly being who brings His message to a person (Genesis 19:15-17; Acts 12:6-9). In addition, no angelic being from heaven will ever have to stand before their Creator and be responsible to Him for the condition of the Church on earth…only those who have been entrusted with the gospel of His Son and the care of His sheep (Jeremiah 3:15; Acts 20:28; 2 Corinthians 8:23).

So it is easy to distinguish the difference and clearly see in these two chapters that the word *angel* refers to a man and not to an angelic being. These seven *angels,* then, are men who had been called by the Spirit of God into an apostolic or pastoral leadership role within the local churches mentioned. Some have thought this word referred to postal carriers who delivered the messages to the churches. However, in Revelation 1:16, these messengers are being held in the grip of their glorified Christ. His grip is His proclamation that they will be held accountable to Him for the spiritual condition of the churches they are shepherding and, as such, with a stricter judgment, something a postal carrier would not be (Luke 16:1-2; Matthew 25:14-30). Although a traveling missionary may have, in fact, delivered these seven messages for John to the messengers themselves, Christ's message is directed in a very pointed way first and foremost to the apostolic or pastoral leader within each church and then out to their congregation at large. The *"you"* then can be read as both singular and plural since sheep are a reflection of the care of the shepherd! Much like a pebble thrown on the surface of a pool of water, each message is to have its ripple effect: first touching the messenger's heart, then the hearts of the members of his congregation, and then out to the other churches as well. Each of the Lord Jesus' messages speaks pointedly to wherever there is a need for praise, correction, rebuke, exhortation, and encouragement (Galatians 2:11-14; 1 Timothy 6:11-14; 20-21).

Now listen to the Father's heart from Watchman Nee's book, *The Normal Christian Life*:

> "When we think of sin, we instinctively think of the judgment it brings; we invariably associate it with condemnation and hell. Man's thought is always of the punishment that will come to him if he sins, but God's thought is always of the glory man will miss if he sins. The result of sin is that we forfeit God's glory; the result of redemption is that we are qualified again for glory. God's purpose in redemption is glory, glory, glory." (Nee, April 2007, p.69-70).

2 Timothy 3:16-17 also lends itself in further hearing our Father's heartbeat in these messages: *All Scripture is inspired by God and profitable for teaching, for reproof, for correction,* ***for training in righteousness;*** *so that the man of God may be adequate, equipped for every good work.* [emphasis added]

Now that we have these two perspectives and are more deeply positioned in spirit, let us

...hear what the Spirit says to the churches...

Chapter One:
Something Is Missing

The Revelation of Jesus Christ starts building upon itself in Chapter 1 with the Lord Jesus' personal manifestation of Himself to John while on the island of Patmos as the Living One. John's spiritual eyes were opened with that manifestation; having been prepared in spirit, John then receives the Lord's personal messages to the seven messengers as recorded in Chapters Two and Three. Through these seven messages, God the Father is actually going to begin a deeper strengthening of His children as their Vinedresser by lifting up and cutting away the debris of empty opinions and the innuendoes of false teachings that had crept into His Son's church…just as the apostle Paul said they would in his farewell to the church at Ephesus (John 15:1-4; Acts 20:29-31). Within these two chapters, the Holy Spirit brings each messenger and the churches and the Church herself into a greater depth of understanding of what it takes to remain true to their risen and ascended Lord at any cost. All hear God's call anew to stay up higher in spirit as the Holy Spirit brings them more fully into the reality of who the Father's eternal Son truly is, of who they are in Him, and of what He has already secured for them and expects of them through His incarnation, death, resurrection, ascension, and exaltation. For herein we will soon discover the loving heart of our heavenly Father just as the Lord Jesus said in Revelation 3:19: *Those whom I love, I reprove and discipline; therefore be zealous and repent.* (Psalm 94:12-13; Hebrews 12:11).

> ***To the angel of the church of Ephesus write:*** *The One who holds the seven stars in His right hand, the One who walks among the seven golden lampstands, says this: "I know your deeds and your toil and perseverance, and that you cannot tolerate evil men, and you put to the test those who call themselves apostles, and they are not, and you found them to be false; and you have perseverance and have endured for My name's sake, and have not grown weary. But I have this against you, that you have left your first love. Therefore remember from where you have fallen, and repent and do the deeds you did at first; or else I am coming to you and will remove your lampstand out of its place—unless you repent. Yet this you do have, that you hate the deeds of the Nicolaitans, which I also hate. He who has an ear, let him hear what the Spirit says to the churches. To him who overcomes, I will grant to eat of the tree of life which is in the Paradise of God.* **Revelation 2:1-7**

Stop just for a moment and reflectively consider the church of Ephesus—the first of the seven churches mentioned in Chapters 2 and 3. The apostle Paul, who laid its foundation upon his return to them from his second missionary trip, then wrote them a circular letter while he was imprisoned and awaiting trial in Rome. His letter is surely one of the highest mountain peaks of revelation in all the Holy Scriptures. Within it, the Holy Spirit unveiled for them what had been revealed to him…a breathtaking picture of God's mystery and its manifold wisdom in His purpose for the world through His Son and His Bride, the Church. In the eternal mind of the Father, her relationship to His eternal Son has always been that of a Bride! And as such, she is to be a reflection of her Bridegroom's ascension glory during His absence and until His return. As a glorious Church, she is also to be a ministering

Church alongside Him in the heavenly places extending His victory out over every kind of evil while she is advancing His Kingdom here on earth. This truth, along with other facets of it, had been illuminated to the church of Ephesus by the Holy Spirit in her earlier years, and now is the backdrop for what the Lord Jesus says to its messenger (Ephesians 1:19-23; 6:10-12).

The Lord's message to this messenger begins with a commendation: He sees his works…his genuine undertakings in examining those who are making themselves out to be His apostles and yet are not, the weariness that endeavor has cost him, and his perseverance in not succumbing to its various pressures both from within and without. Indeed, he has not shrunk away from that work, not even for a minute, for the sake of His name.

Even so, this messenger is in a state of deception. This becomes obvious when you realize he is unaware of his fallen state (verse 5a)! What had happened here? Having first entertained and believed the lie, he then stepped down into its error over a period of time. Now living an external life of mere religiosity (a form of godliness empty of true life and its power), he is unaware and oblivious that he had only an outward appearance of Christian living and ministry, not its inward reality. And isn't that what happened to Adam and Eve in the Garden of Eden after their own fall from God's high estate for them? (Genesis 3:7; 2 Corinthians 11:2-3).

The living One, who holds the seven stars in His right hand and stands in the midst of the seven golden candlesticks inspecting these churches, uses bridal language in pinpointing the true issue at hand for this messenger. He admonishes him with these words: *But I have this against you, that you have left your first love.* Those words, *first love,* refer to the exclusive love of a bride and a bridegroom for each other: a devoted love to one another so deep and so wide that it involves the very deepest affections of their hearts toward each other. Like a lovesick bride who earnestly longs for the companionship of her bridegroom, the Bride's soul is to be a thirst for the living God as First Love (1 John 4:19, Galatians 2:20).

> *O God, Thou art My God; early will I seek Thee: my soul thirsteth for Thee, my flesh longeth for Thee, in a dry and weary land, where no water is; to see Thy power and Thy glory, so as I have seen Thee in the sanctuary. Because Thy lovingkindness is better than life, my lips shall praise Thee. Thus I will bless Thee while I live; I will lift up my hands in Thy name. My soul shall be satisfied as with marrow and fatness, and my mouth shall praise Thee with joyful lips: when I remember Thee upon my bed, and meditate on Thee in the night watches. Because Thou hast been my help, therefore in the shadow of Thy wings will I rejoice. My soul followeth hard after Thee: Thy right hand upholdeth me.*
> Psalm 63:1-8 KJV.

The Lord's selection of the word *left* in Revelation 2:4 is also another bridal term, and its significance probes more deeply into the heart of this messenger. It is a compound word that means "to send away from oneself, to dismiss." It also means "to neglect, forsake, leave alone." The word is a reflection of what actually happens in a divorce. The Lord Jesus is saying then that this messenger has dismissed—neglected, forsaken, and left alone Him as First Love. Another way of saying that is to say that he has been unfaithful to Him as a wife. Do you remember Jesus' answer to a young expert in the Mosaic Law who put Him to the test with his question of what commandment is the first of all? Hear His answer: *The first of all the commandments is, Hear, O Israel; the LORD our God is one LORD: and you shall love the LORD your God with all thy heart, and with all thy soul, and with all thy mind, and with all thy strength: this is the first commandment.* Mark 12:29-30 KJV The word *all* is what is missing in this messenger's relationship with his Bridegroom! The love that once burned in his heart for Christ alone was now but embers. Perhaps he had forgotten his Lord's words of greeting to Mary when she turned around from looking into His empty tomb. Now her risen Lord, He said to her, *Whom are you seeking?* John 20:15

Distracted and no longer focused in spirit, the messenger of the church of Ephesus is living far below his proper position and calling in his spiritual life: *But God, being rich in mercy because of His great love with which He loved us, even when we were dead in our transgressions, made us alive together with Christ (by grace you have been saved), and raised us up with Him, and seated us with Him in the heavenly places in Christ Jesus.* Ephesians 2:4-6

In the light of that truth, the Lord Jesus Christ then admonishes him in verse 5 with His words: *Remember therefore from whence thou hast fallen, and repent, and do the first works.* He redirects his gaze back to Him at his side in the heavenly places first and then brings him full circle by using more bridal language with His use of the words *first works*. You may be wondering now what that could be and how they are connected with where this messenger had fallen from.

The Lord's Supper is a covenant meal and was instituted by Him amazingly on the evening before His crucifixion with the past, present, and future in mind for His people. At this communion table each true believer has been brought into union with their

Lord Jesus through the regenerating work of the Holy Spirit at the moment of their conversion. This memorial time is a set apart time of remembrance for His Bride of the new covenant of peace which she has entered into, and of His covenant love for her and hers for Him, and of the future Kingdom of God upon His return. It is a sacred time in which each one may sit quietly in communion with Him as their Bridegroom and He with them as His Bride, and in a most special way. As Host of the table, He is present with her in the most intimate of ways: here each may pour out their heartfelt love and devotion and adoration in thanksgiving and praises and worship to Him as her risen and soon coming exalted King! And together they may arise in agreement with Him and one another, united in purpose and ready to serve alongside one another.

Listen now to the message Hezekiah sent to all Israel and Judah in their backslidden condition, and what had been found missing in their lives.

> *So they established a decree to circulate a proclamation throughout all Israel from Beersheba even to Dan, that they should **come to celebrate the Passover to the LORD God of Israel** at Jerusalem. For they had not celebrated it in great numbers as it was prescribed. The couriers went throughout all Israel and Judah with the letters from the hand of the king and his princes, even according to the command of the king, saying, O sons of Israel return to the LORD God of Abraham, Isaac, and Israel, that He may return to those of you who escaped and are left from the hand of the kings of Assyria. Do not be like your fathers and your brothers, who were unfaithful to the LORD God of their fathers, so that He made them a horror as you see.*

> *Now do not stiffen your neck like your fathers, but **yield to the LORD and enter His sanctuary which He has consecrated forever**, and **serve** the LORD your God, that His burning anger may turn away from you.* 2 Chronicles 30:5-8 [emphasis added]

We also have Paul's admonition from 1 Corinthians 11:23-27.

> *For I received from the Lord that which I also delivered to you, that the Lord Jesus in the night in which He was betrayed took bread; and when He had given thanks, He broke it and said, This is My body, which is for you; do this in remembrance of Me. In the same way He took the cup also after supper, saying, This cup is the new covenant in My blood; do this, as often as you drink it, in remembrance of Me. For as often as you eat this bread and drink the cup, **you proclaim the Lord's death until He comes.*** [emphasis added]

When Jesus reclined at the table with His apostles for what would be their last Passover meal together until His return, He shared with them His heart's desire for fellowship with them and among themselves with these words: *I have earnestly desired to eat this Passover **with you** before I suffer.* [emphasis added] That hasn't changed. Sadly though, years later Paul had to admonish the church at Corinth about that centrality and importance of the Lord's Supper. Obviously, something had happened; in fact, something was missing! So, too, for the messenger of the church in Ephesus and his congregation. Although he may have practiced the outward form of the Lord's supper with them as a community of believers in some way or another in the church's gathering times, its significance had greatly paled for him along with its intended purpose (1 Corinthians 10:16-17; Philippians 2:1-2). Rather than taking time to hold their communion in a place of highest priority and in a manner worthy of His holy name and presence, it had become to him, and thus for them, more of a tradition done out of habit…or even as an inconvenience or encumbrance…rather than the center and substance of life in their gatherings (Luke 22:4-21; 1 Corinthians 5:6-8).

By God's design, each member of the body of Christ, the Church, has entered once and for all into the Holy of Holies, Christ Jesus Himself being that. Here the bride of Christ may look fully into the glorious and wondrous face of her Passover Lamb as First Love…and therein be richly filled and satisfied with Him and His love for her! Without such spiritual intimacy alone with Him in the secret place of His personal presence and without such rest in Him, there can be little illumination in her spirit of her sovereign Lord, little true worship of Him alone, and little true obedience to Him on her part. For from His table of covenant blessing where the sacrificial elements are laid out before her, she may now arise to trust in her God as never before and go forth in spirit and truth into the world with the beauty and power of her ascended Lord and Savior within her and upon her (Isaiah 60:1-4).

Sadly, having failed to discern himself and the body of Christ properly and how it is designed to function through community, the reality of Christ Himself within the messenger of the church in Ephesus and the congregants is but a dim memory! (1 Corinthians 5:6-8)

Should you be tempted to think all of this is but a light issue and rebuke, only to this messenger does his glorified Lord say that He will come quickly and remove his lamp from the Candlestick unless he repents deeply. And yet, in the midst of this strong rebuke, there's light and hope in verse 6! This messenger's heart and thoughts had remained inwardly in agreement with his Lord's regarding the Nicolaitans. For that, the Lord gives him praise. For like Him, he, too, detests their works—reprobates who entice and seduce His people by practicing fornication and eating things sacrificed to idols while at the same time outwardly professing themselves to be Christians…and in that way dragging those weak in faith along with them into their sin! (Romans 1:28-32).

CHAPTER TWO:
In The Face of Persecution

> **And to the angel of the church in Smyrna write:** *The first and the last, who was dead, and has come to life, says this: "I know your tribulation and your poverty (but you are rich), and the blasphemy by those who say they are Jews and are not, but are a synagogue of Satan. Do not fear what you are about to suffer. Behold, the devil is about to cast some of you into prison, so that you will be tested, and you will have tribulation for ten days. Be faithful unto death, and I will give you the crown of life. He who has an ear, let him hear what the Spirit says to the churches. He who overcomes will not be hurt by the second death."*
> **Revelation 2:8-11**

Smyrna was a commercial city along a well-known ancient trade route. So it is likely the gospel of Christ's glory reached it from the church of Ephesus during its early days. At the time of this letter, the messenger of the church in Smyrna was encountering fierce opposition from those who said they were Jews but, in truth, were not. As always, these Jews were in bitter opposition to Jesus Christ and anyone who claimed loyalty to Him (John 8:37-38; 1 Thessalonians 2:13-15).

This brings us directly to the first point. The messenger of the church in Smyrna is in a state of the tension that comes with fiery persecution—of being both harassed and oppressed through various kinds of ill-treatment because of his fidelity to his risen

Lord and Savior Jesus Christ and His gospel message of God's Kingdom. He is suffering physically and mentally for what he knows to be true and right about Him, as well as himself as His gospel messenger. Thus, the Lord begins His message to him with these illuminating words, *the first and the last, who was dead and has come to life.* Here the Lord Jesus reiterates and amplifies for him the reality of His own personal death and resurrection, having Himself conquered and abolished death in His own body once and for all on the Cross. For it was through His vicarious death there on the Cross for mankind that his Lord had indeed robbed death of its sting: *For since by a man came death, by a man also came the resurrection from the dead…who abolished death and brought life and immortality to light through the gospel.* 1 Corinthians 15:21; 2 Timothy 1:10

This messenger has stood the fiery test of persecution…he has stayed the course and come to know these truths beyond any shadow of doubt, not only of Him but of how they applied to his own life as well…in the same way the deacon Stephen knew when he was facing martyrdom. This messenger would not shrink back from death but would preach the gospel in its fullness…its beginning and its end! (Philippians 2:6-11; 1 Thessalonians 4:13-17; Revelation 21:1-4; 22-23).

Being unashamed of his Lord's testimony, this messenger's church was not a silent church either. Faith in their risen and ascended and exalted Christ, with all of its implications, had emboldened him and them to speak up in the face of adversity and persecution from truths that had anchored their souls well in the faith of the gospel and the hope that accompanies it. *But having the same spirit of faith, according to what is written, "I BELIEVED, THEREFORE I SPOKE", we also believe, therefore we also speak, knowing that He who raised the Lord Jesus will raise us also with Jesus and will present us with you.* 2 Corinthians 4:13-14

This messenger knew his holy calling here and the future of the redeemed. With such a belief structure and focus, he remained single-minded in serving His Lord.

> *But I do not consider my life of any account as dear to myself, so that I may finish my course and the ministry which I received from the Lord Jesus, to testify solemnly of the gospel of the grace of God. For this reason I also suffer these things, but I am not ashamed; for I know whom I have believed and I am convinced that He is able to guard what I have entrusted to Him until that day.* Acts 20:24

He also believed what Jesus said to Martha in the face of her own brother's death:

> *Your brother will rise again. Martha said to Him, I know that he will rise on the last day. Jesus said to her, I am the resurrection and the life; he who believes in Me will live even if he dies, and everyone who lives and believes in Me will never die. Do you believe this?* John 11:25-26

This messenger believed it! Physical death was no longer a mystery to him. It had no hold on him, for he understood it as being his servant and a gateway to his final entrance into glory and all of its bliss and its unspeakable joy (Revelation 14:13).

The Lord Jesus had no rebuke for this messenger. With eyes that see past the externals of what the world calls poverty, the Lord sees him as he truly is—blessed in and with Him. For the messenger of the church in Smyrna, even under the most pressing of circumstances, had indeed taken hold of that which is true life and had not let go of his promised inheritance...*the wealth that comes from the full assurance of understanding, resulting in a true knowledge of God's mystery, that is Christ Himself, in whom are hidden all the treasures of wisdom and knowledge.* Colossians 2:2a-3

Now you can see more clearly why this particular messenger had such a high commendation from His Lord and was indeed a proven bondservant of Him as the exalted Christ! A bondservant at this time was a servant by choice...a slave who, having been granted freedom by his master, loved him so deeply that he voluntarily chose to be his servant until death. In the light of this and of the promise of more intense persecutions ahead of him, the Lord pointedly uses more bridal language in His exhortation to this messenger with His words *faithful unto death*. That is the depth of what a bridegroom and bride pledge themselves to when they exchange their marriage vows before each other. It is another way of saying they will not allow anything to come between them except death (2 Timothy 1:8-12).

Watchman Nee says it ever so well in his book, The Normal Christian Life.

> "Lord, I am willing to let go all of this for You: not just for Your work, not for Your children, not for anything else at all, but altogether for Yourself.

> Oh, to be wasted! It is a blessed thing to be wasted for the Lord. So many who have been prominent in the Christian world know nothing of this. Many of us have been used to the full—have been used, I would say, too much—but we do not know what it means to be wasted on God. We like to be "always on the go": the Lord would sometimes prefer to have us in prison. We think in terms of apostolic journeys: God dares to put His greatest ambassadors in chains." (Nee, April 2007, p.188).

And so in the very midst of such intense tribulations and persecution, and with more to come, the Alpha and Omega calls to His Bride to fulfill her vow to Him in the deepest way… up to the very point of death. What that means is that in spite of the sacrifices she will have to make and any perils she may have to face and endure for her profession and proclamation of Him as the Christ, she is to guard with her very life the true gospel of His Kingdom glory and maintain her faith and stance in Him at all times.

This messenger had heard that call and answered it well. Having laid down his life before Him and giving Him his Yes, he is consistently living his life at that level of faith and commitment… he is living for the glory of His name alone! (Matthew 10:24-25; 1 Corinthians 10:31-33; Colossians 1:24-25).

CHAPTER THREE:
Stop Being Silent

> **And to the angel of the church in Pergamos write:** *The One who has the sharp two-edged sword says this: "I know where you dwell, where Satan's throne is; and you hold fast My name, and did not deny My faith even in the days of Antipas, My witness, My faithful one, who was killed among you, where Satan dwells. But I have a few things against you, because you have there some who hold the teaching of Balaam, who kept teaching Balak to put a stumbling block before the sons of Israel, to eat things sacrificed to idols and to commit acts of immorality. So you also have some who in the same way hold the teaching of the Nicolaitans. Therefore repent; or else I am coming to you quickly, and I will make war against them with the sword of My mouth. He who has an ear, let him hear what the Spirit says to the churches. To him who overcomes, to him I will give some of the hidden manna, and I will give him a white stone, and a new name written on the stone which no one knows but he who receives it."* **Revelation 2:12-17**

Under the Holy Spirit's inspiration, the church in this city is third in order because of a divine sequence being mapped out for the reader. Besides being a city of temples and pagan cults devoted to sensuous worship, which was nothing unusual for cities in those days, Pergamos was also the seat of Roman emperor worship…meaning he was being worshiped there as being divine. That was considered to be the hallmark of civic loyalty at that time. However, the One who has the two-edged sword sees it for what it really is: it is where Satan has enthroned himself and is being worshipped.

We know from the whole counsel of the Bible that God must act in harmony with His nature and His very own perfections. We also know that whenever He has been repeatedly provoked to anger, He will then move swiftly in His righteous judgment. That is why the Lord Jesus addresses the messenger of the church in Pergamos as *The One who has the sharp two-edged sword.* Those last words are an abbreviated way of saying the sharp two-edged sword of judgment. Jesus is revealing Himself to this messenger as the Righteous Judge. Having already heard the case, He now proceeds to render a proper verdict (Deuteronomy 32:16-18; Acts 5:1-11).

Even though this messenger had indeed taken hold of and held fast the Lord's name and had not turned away and rejected his faith in Him even in the days of Antipas the martyr, he is in a state of passivity and negligence, having been reticent to stand up for the truth with a righteous voice. Sin is in the camp! There are some in the congregation who are holding to the teaching of Balaam and are enticing and leading others into the same kind of fornication and licentiousness that he had. A jealous God, the LORD is never passive towards sin as some may think. The time will come when He will judge it in any of its various forms and manifestations for what it really is—idolatry. His righteous standard has never changed: *And there is no other God before Me, a righteous God and a Savior; there is none except Me.* Isaiah 45:21b

In King Nebuchadnezzar's days, three young Hebrew men took a stand for the Lord God. At the cost of their lives, they refused to serve his gods by bowing down and worshipping the golden image he had fashioned and set up. This messenger is in a similar crisis, especially given the city he is in. It's a question of worship: who will he worship? Would he, as a follower of Christ and a pastoral/apostolic leader, compromise the truth by not taking the action needed in order to avoid conflict? In his pride, had he forgotten or ignored the truth that it only takes a little leaven to leaven the whole lump of dough? It would do him well to remember the truth Paul wrote to the church in Corinth: *What do I mean then? That a thing sacrificed to idols is anything, or that an idol is anything? No, but I say that the things which the Gentiles sacrifice, they sacrifice to demons. You cannot drink the cup of the Lord and the cup of demons; you cannot partake of the table of the Lord and the table of demons. Or do we provoke the Lord to jealousy? We are not stronger than He, are we?* 1 Corinthians 10:19-22

In the Old Testament, Balaam was a prophet for hire. Unable to curse God's people directly as requested by King Balak, he taught the king to put a stumbling block before the sons of Israel…one that would cause them to fall away from the living God and in this way bring a curse upon them. The result of Balaam's counsel was that Balak successfully seduced the men of Israel into compromise through the pagan women of Moab and, in this way, they fell away from their God and played the harlot. In verse 15, you can hear the gavel of God's judgment in His words, *in the same way*. Instead of bringing a rebuke, this messenger was playing it safe by allowing those within his congregation who were adhering to the false teaching of the Nicolaitans to go unchallenged. It surely is the goodness of the Lord God that leads one to repent of their sin. Had He left it unchecked, the result of his continued indulging of this fleshly passivity would have not only been a loss of reverence for his God but the inability to recognize true greatness for what it really is. *He has told you, O man, what is good; and what does the LORD require of you but to do justice, to love kindness, and to walk humbly with your God.* Micah 6:8

The temple where God dwells on earth now is no longer the fabrication or work of a man's hand: a mere building or edifice. It cannot be so. For under the new covenant of peace which was ratified by Christ's shed blood on the Cross, God's dwelling place on earth is His people. Since the day of Pentecost, His temple now is made of living stones—those who have actually believed in Jesus' Name and been born of His Spirit. Each one is where God dwells and meets them and is worshipped. The Holy Spirit within them makes His house of residence a holy one. Being one spirit with the Lord Jesus, He speaks and moves within them by His Spirit in power. Just as in the Old Testament, the glory of the LORD filled His tabernacle, so it is to be individually and collectively as members of Christ's mystical body on earth. It is from here in glory that the Church is to proclaim the true gospel of the enthroned Christ while demonstrating His power on earth through the Holy Spirit (Acts 15:15-18; 1 Peter 2:4-5; Ephesians 2:20-22; Psalm 24:7-10).

The glorified Christ, the One who has that sharp two-edged sword, is coming again for a pure Bride who is without a spot or blemish. As such, her doctrine is to be pure and holy in the same way. After all, a stewardship has been entrusted to her. Nothing polluted is to enter in through her door which would encroach upon the Lord's enthronement in glory, thereby bringing a reproach on His holy Name. That stewardship is like a pillar, one that has been set on a firm foundation standing from top to bottom alone, supporting the building by carrying its weight. Like that pillar, the Church's primary responsibility, as well as this messenger's, is to guard and preserve the truth of the gospel of Jesus Christ and the apostolic teaching of the New Testament apostles. Consider here the example that had been given to him by John the Baptist in the gospels of Matthew and Mark (Matthew 3:7-10; Luke 3:18-20). Did you notice there that John was not a reed shaken by the wind? Instead, like a strong pillar that neither bends nor sways, he steadfastly refused to compromise God's Word and His prophetic call to him. It was in this light that he preached His commandments without fear of others. John never yielded to the popular opinions of his day, regardless of who or what they were…or what it would cost him.

And just like him, the Church is not to be a reed shaken by the wind! As the pillar of truth in the earth, she is to stand with her God against any sin and false doctrine of any kind. She is to proclaim His Word steadfastly without fear of what others may think or say or do. She must refuse to compromise the truth found in the Bible and be quick to refute errors of any kind. She must also carefully test any teaching or activity attempting to make its way in and the spirit of it. Does the teaching bear the same kind of spirit and emphasis as the Lord Jesus and the apostles in the New Testament? And what about the life of the preacher/teacher? Are they living their life under the Lordship of Jesus Christ? What about their relationship to the spirit of this age that tries to undermine the authority of God's Word and the Church? And what about their relation to the ungodly world in which they live? Are they living a separated life?

In this way, the Church demonstrates her absolute fidelity to her Lord and Savior Jesus Christ…unlike the religious authorities in John's day who ignored Herod's sin in silence; and unlike this messenger of the church in Pergamos during the days of Antipas the martyr!

Chapter Four:
Deal with Jezebel

And to the angel of the church in Thyatira write:
The Son of God, who has eyes (lit. His eyes) like a flame of fire, and His feet are like burnished bronze, says this: "I know your deeds, and your love and faith and service and perseverance, and that your deeds of late are greater than at first. But I do have this against you, that you tolerate the woman Jezebel, who calls herself a prophetess, and she teaches and leads My bondservants astray so that they commit acts of immorality and eat things sacrificed to idols. I gave her time to repent, and she does not want to repent of her immorality. Behold, I will throw her on a bed of sickness, and those who commit adultery with her into great tribulation, unless they repent of her deeds. And I will kill her children with pestilence (lit. death), and all the churches will know that I am He who searches the minds (lit. inner man) and hearts; and I will give to each one of you according to your deeds. But I say to you, the rest who are in Thyatira, who do not hold this teaching, who have not known the deep things of Satan, as they call them—I place no other burden on you. Nevertheless what you have, hold fast until I come. He who overcomes, and he who keeps My deeds until the end, TO HIM I WILL GIVE AUTHORITY OVER THE NATIONS: AND HE SHALL RULE (Lit. shepherd) THEM WITH A ROD OF IRON, AS THE VESSELS OF THE POTTER ARE BROKEN TO PIECES, as I also have received authority from My Father; and I will give him the morning star. He

> *who has an ear, let him hear what the Spirit says to the churches."* **Revelation 2:18-29**

The Son of God, who has His eyes like a flame of fire and His feet are like burnished bronze is the Son made perfect forever. The word *perfect* means to accomplish, to carry through to the end, to make perfect by reaching the intended goal. In Hebrews 7:28, the thought in *the Son made perfect forever* is that Jesus Christ remained obedient to His Father's will even in the most pressing of hardships, temptations, and sufferings. He followed this path of testing in His earthly life right up to its appointed end of death on a cross, having never sinned. That perfecting of Christ was one in which He as a Man consistently chose good and refused evil. The second Adam, He thus proved Himself to be fit not only as the Savior of all who would believe in Him but also as the Judge of all the people. Having taken on and successfully fulfilled God's full judgment against sin in His own body on the cross, the glorified Son is addressing the messenger of the church of Thyatira as the last Adam…the perfect Man and Judge of all (1 Corinthians 15:20-26; 45-47; Acts 17:30-31).

In spite of his deeds, his love and faith, his service and perseverance, and that his present ministering of divine things (like the priests in the holy place) is greater than his first, the messenger of the church in Thyatira is in a state of indifference. As the shepherd of His flock and the spiritual leader of this church, he has shown no concern about teaching in it that is blatantly opposed to and contrary to God's standard of righteousness and the gospel of Christ. For within his congregation, there is unrighteous, unbiblical, and heretical teaching by one of its own spiritual leaders! To be specific (which He always is), this messenger has been closing his eyes to *the woman Jezebel*—one who calls herself a prophetess yet is teaching and leading the Lord's bondservants away from the very faith which has saved them. Just like the Jezebel who was married to Ahab the king of Israel did, and through her cunning, became its virtual ruler. It's time for this messenger to wake up! The Lord Jesus' use of the words here, *the woman Jezebel,* is an Old Testament word picture that points to idolatry, sensuality, and manipulative control. It is used especially about someone, male or female, who misrepresents and twists the truth in such a way as to seductively gain freedom for God's people to sin. That Jezebel, and the demonic spirit behind it, is actually functioning unchallenged by him in a leadership position of preaching and teaching within the local church in Thyatira!

Listen now to what the Holy Spirit had already alerted this messenger to:

> *Be on guard for yourselves and for all the flock, among which the Holy Spirit has made you overseers, to shepherd the church of God which He purchased with His own blood. I know that after my departure savage wolves will come in among you, not sparing the flock; and from among your own selves men will arise, speaking perverse things, to draw away the disciples after them. For certain persons have crept in unnoticed, those who were long beforehand marked out for this condemnation, ungodly persons who turn the grace of God into licentiousness and deny our only Master and Lord Jesus Christ.* Acts 20: 28-30; Jude 4

Everything is open and laid bare before the eyes of the Son of God, which are depicted here as flames of fire. In the sacred

Scriptures, fire is often symbolic of judgment and purification. Fire tests precious metals so that any dross in them surfaces and can then be removed. The Lord's righteous judgments are like that fire: they especially purify the faith of the impurities of pride and the unbelief that comes along with it. The intensity of His judgments makes necessary distinctions and separate out for us that which is true from that which is false, and that which is holy from that which is ungodly, and that which is eternal from that which is temporal. Having passed through the purifying fire Himself as a Man without any taint of sin, the Son of God's holy jealousy and righteous anger and judgment now burns within Him against those who defile His holiness and depart from His righteous ways into various forms of idolatry (Jeremiah 17:9-10; Hebrews 12:25-*27).*

There is yet another bridal thought that comes into play here when we understand more deeply who God truly is. Always holy and righteous, His jealousy is the same kind of holy jealousy that guards the affections and love of one spouse to the other in the marriage union of a man and a woman. Marriage partners rightfully expect exclusive love and loyalty to each other and require in a holy way that each remain completely faithful and true to the other in their marriage vows and relationship. The Son of God (verse 18) is making it known to this messenger that He is no different! The Son's jealousy is His holy intolerance for anything that can divide the affections of this messenger's heart towards Him and His Father, and in this way forfeit His Father's blessing for him and the people he is shepherding. For the Lord Jesus Christ passionately desires that His people come into the fullness of an intimate knowledge of who their heavenly Father is and who they are as His children (Galatians 4:4-7).

Listen carefully:

Now if any man builds on the foundation with gold, silver, precious stones, wood, hay, straw, each man's work will become evident; for the day will show it because it is to be revealed with fire, and the fire itself will test the quality of each man's work (lit. of what sort each man's work is). If any man's work which he has built on it remains, he will receive a reward. If any man's work is burned up, he will suffer loss; but he himself will be saved, yet so as through fire. Do you not know that you are a temple of God and that the Spirit of God dwells in you? If any man destroys the temple of God, God will destroy him; for the temple of God is holy, and that is what you are (lit. who you are). 1 Corinthians 3:12-17

Beware of the false prophets who come to you in sheep's clothing, but inwardly are ravenous wolves. You will know them by their fruits. Grapes are not gathered from thorn bushes nor figs from thistles, are they? So every good tree bears good fruit, but the bad tree bears bad fruit. A good tree cannot produce bad fruit, nor can a bad tree produce good fruit. Every tree that does not bear good fruit is cut down and thrown into the fire. So then, you will know them by their fruits. Not everyone who says to Me, Lord, Lord, will enter the kingdom of heaven, but he who does the will of My Father who is in heaven will enter. Many will say to Me on that day, Lord, Lord, did we not prophesy in Your name, and in Your name cast out demons, and in Your name perform many miracles? And then I will declare to them, I never knew you; Depart from Me, you who practice lawlessness. Matthew 7:15-23

Did you hear in those scriptures that God is not a respecter of persons? It means it's impossible for Him to show partiality to a person in any one of His judgments. Being both perfect in love and justice, He cannot leave the guilty go unpunished regardless of who the person is or is not…nor can He not reward the deeds of the righteous regardless of their station in life. No one is overlooked by Him. That truth is threaded throughout the Old and New Testaments, and it is intended to bring someone into either trembling or gratitude within them…whichever the case may be (Job 34:10-12; Romans 2:4-11; 1 Peter 1:17-19).

Once handed down, the Son's judgment is swiftly executed with a purpose in mind. Like Pharaoh in the book of Exodus, *the woman Jezebel* in the church in Thyatira has willfully and repeatedly refused to repent of her sin at every gracious opportunity God has given her to do so. Time has run out. The Son of God says He will throw her into a bed of sickness; and that He will also throw those who have been committing spiritual adultery with her into great tribulation…unless they repent of her deeds. Did you notice the word *her* there? That's how far they had fallen into sin and how serious it was. And His judgment doesn't end there. He will also kill her spiritual children with death. For the One who is holy and true rightfully gives to each one according to their works. Indeed, it is a terrifying thing to fall into the hands of the living God!

The Son's words in verse 23—*and all the churches will know that I am He who searches the minds and the hearts; and* I *will give to each one according to your deed*—sits square center in the very middle of the seven messages to the seven churches, much like the epicenter of an earthquake where a seismic rupture begins. The Son of God who has eyes like a flame of fire and feet like burnished bronze is going to move by His Spirit in this church as her Judge so swiftly and deal with its sin so thoroughly that no one will mistake His sovereignty in having done so! His words then are a strong word of exhortation and reproof to this messenger and are intended by Him to bring him around to a holy fear of God: one that actually strikes one speechless with humbleness of mind and heart and genuine repentance of their sin. The fact that He does not instruct this messenger to repent of his sin for tolerating *the woman Jezebel* and her spiritual offspring in the church does not mean that this messenger didn't need to. Jesus' strong words of reproof and His pending judgment of her and them had accomplished that for him. The Lord is directing him and the rest in Thyatira who hadn't held to and practiced the woman Jezebel's teaching, and thereby came to know the deep things of Satan, to consider the deeper issue at hand.

God's righteous judgments bring about not only His justice but its accountability as well. Every preacher and teacher of God's Word, and their congregations, should be especially alert here and take heed. Out of his anger, Moses seriously compromised God's direct word to him by disobeying Him before His people at the waters of Meribah. He did not treat the LORD his God as holy there before their eyes. His judgment for that sin was that Moses would not enter into the promised land of Canaan. Even though Moses would later entreat Him with strong pleadings to change His mind, God stoutly refused his plea because of the seriousness of his sin before His people. Moses would only see Canaan from a distance and not cross over the Jordan river into it with them as their leader. King David and the death of Uzzah is another example of God's righteous judgments in a leader's life. Through David's own irreverence and misplaced enthusiasm in bringing up the ark of the Divine Presence to Jerusalem, another man sinned and died for it. That is a sobering thought indeed! And it took that to bring an about-face for David…

one in which he learned a very humbling and sobering lesson in accountability to his God as the spiritual leader of His people (Deuteronomy 3:23-27; 2 Samuel 6:1-11).

Leaders in the church have been entrusted with guarding the true gospel of Christ and with being examples of righteous living to His flock. In the grip of His hand, the Son of God (whose eyes are like a flame of fire and His feet like burnished bronze) is continually evaluating their ministry, character, and stand against sin and evil…and with a stricter judgment. After all, to whomever much is given, much is required. For where the shepherd goes, the sheep follow. Paul wrote to the churches of Galatia addressing the issue at hand for this messenger in a still deeper way. *For am I now seeking the favor of men, or of God? Or am I striving to please men? If I were still striving to please men, I would not be a bondservant of Christ.* Galatians 1:10

A spiritual leader's life and ministry have as much potential for harm as it does for good. That is indeed another very sobering thought. It is in the light of this truth that the Lord's stricter judgment for a leader, as well as a church, may mean that the consequences for serious sin will not be removed from them. With this in mind, the Son of God said to this messenger and the rest in Thyatira who were not holding to the teaching of the woman Jezebel, *"…I place no other burden on you…"* He was essentially saying to him and them, deal with the issue and then live accordingly.

That exhortation, if deeply appropriated by this messenger, will instill in him the holy habit of seeking His Lord as His bondservant while living ever so humbly before Him in the care of His flock. Like a fully weaned child leaning against its mother's shoulder, his repentance will be a true one and genuine greatness in the eyes of the living God! (Psalm 131).

CHAPTER FIVE:
On The Verge of Shipwreck

> **To the angel of the church in Sardis write:** *He who has the seven Spirits of God and the seven stars, says this, "I know your deeds, that you have a name that you are alive, but you are dead. Wake up, and strengthen the things that remain, which were about to die; for I have not found your deeds completed in My sight. So remember what (lit. how) you have received and heard; and keep it, and repent. Therefore, if you do not wake up, I will come like a thief, and you will not know at what hour I will come to you. But you have a few people in Sardis who have not soiled their garments; and they walk with Me in white, for they are worthy. He who overcomes will thus be clothed in white garments; and I will not erase his name from the book of life, and I will confess his name before My Father and His angels. He who has an ear, let him hear what the Spirit says to the churches.* **Revelation 3:1-6**

God purposefully placed light bearers in the expanse of the heavens to give light on the earth by day and night. In the time of darkness, the moon and the stars, in a variety of sizes and colors, light up the night sky. God created them by creative design to stand out in the dark country sky to give testimony to Him... of His presence and might and of His glory! (Isaiah 43:10-13).

Now let's listen to how the Lord Jesus addresses the messenger of the church in Sardis. He addresses him as *He who has the seven Spirits of God and the seven stars*. Did the words, *the seven*

Spirits of God, stand out to you? One would want to stop and consider here, "Who is this One who has the seven Spirits of God: what does it mean?"

The number seven in the Bible speaks of sufficiency and completion. As the seventh day began, all of God's work of creation was finished; in other words, His work of creation was now sufficient for the very purpose for which it had been designed! Completed, it was ready to function accordingly. In the same way, when Jesus bowed His head on the Cross and released His human spirit to His heavenly Father, He said, *It is finished.* That transaction there on the Cross wasn't just about our justification through His shed blood. Having met all the demands of Divine holiness by having never sinned in His human body, Jesus subsequently rose bodily from the grave three days later, forever a new Man! His human nature had perfectly met all the heavenly requirements as a vessel for the Divine Presence in its fullness. When Christ then ascended bodily forty days later into heaven, He took that human nature with Him: the one that had been perfected (made complete) and fully sanctified (set apart) on the Cross right up until His last breath. And there in that exaltation before His Father's throne and in His glorious presence, Jesus received from Him the promise made to Him as man's representative: the Spirit of holiness in all of His fullness, a Son made perfect forever! This He did for us so that we too could receive and be filled with the same Holy Spirit, and then live into that same fullness of union and fellowship with Him and His Father (John 7:37-39; Hebrews 7:26-28; John 14:16-20).

This Jesus, being the head of His body, the Church, says to this messenger that He sees his works: he has a name…a title with its public persona of greatness and inflated self-importance…that he's alive. Yet the reality is he's dead: spiritually inactive, inert, and inoperative. Having become a son of God by nature at the very moment of his conversion, he is now in an internal state of spiritual collapse and deterioration…and so is his church. The title he has is a mask that he wears: he has been masquerading, acting like something he is not. Having neglected the great salvation he has in Christ, he has taken on the branding skills and the glitz that come from the world's way of doing things and acting accordingly. By having done so, he is misusing his office… and is misleading the sheep and directing them into that same hypocrisy and debauchery (Matthew 6:24; Jeremiah 23:1-3).

In teaching His disciples during His earthly ministry, Jesus' opening words to them in Matthew 6 were, *Take heed.* KJV Those words were used as strong words of caution for them. To take heed means to hold the mind or the ear toward someone. It involves careful and attentive listening to what someone is about to say because they are going to alert them to a hidden and lurking danger. To take heed is a call to action: reverse your trajectory. It would especially behoove this messenger to take heed! He is way off course.

The fact that this messenger has been masquerading over a period of time says that much of the light within his soul is darkness, and in his case, it is very great! Having failed time and again to remember…to take to heart and reflect on the Christ within him and all its implications…he has missed seeing the true greatness of the God he serves and turned to the world for help. Instead of living the life of faith by the grace of Christ while pressing into the Spirit for truth, there is a lot of mixture in him and the church. Just like King Uzziah, he's unable to discern between what is pure and holy and what is profane. (2 Chronicles 26:16)

This spiritual blindness has increasingly crept into his soul. And with such lack of his own personal transformation, his desires, motives, and preaching have slipped far away from being centered and anchored in Christ alone (Colossians 2:8). Since anything of lasting eternal value must originate with God Himself, the questions then come: In whom is he trusting? Whose work is he doing...his or God's? In the eloquence of simplicity, C.H Spurgeon once said that in the life of faith, neutrality is not an option. You are either ranked under the banner of the Lord Jesus to serve Him and fight His battles His ways, or you are a slave to that dark prince, Satan. Unable to see what's directly in front of him, his life and ministry are falling increasingly short of His eternal destiny for him: the Holy Spirit's fullness in him and his congregation in anticipation of his Lord's promised soon return. What a very sad state of affairs he is in: *I did not send these prophets, but they ran. I did not speak to them, but they prophesied. But if they had stood in My council, then they would have announced My words to My people, and would have turned them back from their evil way and from the evil of their deed.* Jeremiah 23:21-22

Once again, as the shepherd goes, so goes the flock. Bewitched and having ignored multiple corrections, he, and consequently most of the congregation, have been lulled into a false sense of identity and security and are unconcerned...like Samson in the lap of Delilah. Indeed, there are only a few in Sardis who have not defiled their garments of righteousness! Again, what a very sad state of affairs! The green olive tree's branches are close to being dry and worthless: its root system is shallow, and there is little, if any, remaining fruit. The prophet Jeremiah explained it perfectly: *For the shepherds have become stupid and have not sought the LORD; therefore they have not prospered, and all their flock is scattered... Woe to the shepherds who are destroying and scattering the sheep of My pasture, declares the LORD.* Jeremiah 10:21; 23:1

Chapter Five: On The Verge of Shipwreck

This messenger would do well to take heed and step out of his worldliness through a deep repentance for his unfinished works, followed by a deep cleansing that comes through the washing of the water of the Word, and learn Christ. It would also behoove him to learn the parable of the ten virgins…five of whom were foolish, and five of whom were prudent. Taking the position of a servant, immersing himself in the Truth and reflecting upon it with all his heart…the Father can then clip away what is dry and sapless. And he will increasingly be aglow and burning with the Spirit within him. Not only will Light be shining from him, but faith will have arisen in his heart with its power going forth as well. There will no longer be a power shortage in the church (Galatians 3:2-5; James 1:21-25; 1 Thessalonians 2:13).

Knowing the hour, Jesus said to Peter and Zebedee's two sons in the garden of Gethsemane…*remain here and keep watch with Me.* Only to His Bride, the Church, has the risen and exalted Christ given that sacred trust. And only here in the solitude of time spent alone with Him in the Scriptures is her holy fellowship with Him refreshed. Here the heavenly life within her is being renewed and invigorated and strengthened for the day before her. Having been given the authority of the Lord's name and having received the fullness of the Holy Spirit within her from Him, she can wield both the power and the efficacy of prayer: the capacity to produce its desired effect at all levels (James 4:17-18). She is to be found keeping watch and standing in the gap while interceding before Him under the inspiration of the Holy Spirit within her until His promised return for her. It was to those who were buying and selling in the temple that Jesus said these words, *It is written, My house shall be called a house of prayer; but you are making it a robber's den.* Matthew 21:13 Paul also didn't mince any words when he admonished the church at Corinth with these words: *Become sober-minded as you ought, and stop sinning; for some have no knowledge of God. I speak this to your shame.* 1 Corinthians 15:34

As Christ's ambassador for His kingdom on earth, this messenger would indeed do well to take heed of those words, and through a deep repentance for his multifaceted sin, abide by Christ's words alone from this point on! If not, he is at high risk of hearing these words from his Lord on judgment day: *Many will say to me on that day, Lord, did we not prophesy in Your name, and in Your name cast out demons, and in Your name perform many miracles? And then I will declare to them, I never knew you: DEPART FROM ME, YOU WHO PRACTICE LAWLESSNESS.* Matthew 7:22-23

CHAPTER SIX:
Deep Calls to Deep

And to the angel of the church in Philadelphia write: *He who is holy, who is true, who has the key of David, who opens and no one will shut, and who shuts and no one opens, says this: "I know your deeds. Behold, I have put before you an open door which no one can shut, because you have a little power, and have kept My word, and have not denied My name. Behold, I will cause those of the synagogue of Satan, who say that they are Jews and are not, but lie—I will make them come and bow down at your feet, and make them know that I have loved you. Because you have kept the word of My perseverance, I also will keep you from the hour of testing, that hour which is about to come upon the whole world, to test those who dwell on the earth. I am coming quickly; hold fast what you have, so that no one will take your crown. He who overcomes, I will make him a pillar in the temple of My God, and he will not go out from it anymore; and I will write on him the name of My God, and the name of the city of My God, the new Jerusalem which comes down out of heaven from My God, and My new name. He who has an ear, let him hear what the Spirit says to the churches.* **Revelation 3:7-13**

Known unto God are all His works from the beginning of the world. Acts 15:18 KJV What the Lord Jesus is about to say to the messenger of the church in Philadelphia comes from *He who is holy*: meaning, upright and blameless, the purest of the pure, the holy of the holies; or you could say, the holiness of holinesses. He who is Holy is the One *who is true*...the One who has the firmness and the constancy within Himself in keeping and executing His promises and cannot lie. The *Holy* One *who is true* is the promised Seed of the woman, the Root and Descendant of King David...the Anointed One, the Messiah, the Son of God. Having then passed through the heavens bodily into His Father's throne room after His resurrection, Jesus the Christ received from Him there the key to the Messianic Kingdom in recognition of His office as King over all creation in heaven and on earth, and throughout all the universe and its galaxies, and beyond. Having that authority, He has unlimited power at all times, not only over all His creation but in His royal household, the Church, as well. The Bright Morning Star, He is coming again! (Genesis 3:15; 1 Chronicles 17:10b-14; Zechariah 6:12-13; Acts 15:16-18; Revelation 21:22-27).

This One addresses this messenger by saying to him that He sees his works: he has had little achieving power that is his own and has leaned into His Lord for His strength and maintained a watch over His works. And in that work, he has neither refused nor rejected Him as the true Messiah even while finding himself in the midst of Satan's synagogue, those who were saying they were Jews and are liars. In the midst of their jealous insinuations and false accusations, he has followed His Lord's example in suffering and persecution and with a peaceful mind. Another way of saying that comes from 1 Corinthians 4:2: *Moreover it is required in stewards, that a man be found faithful.* This messenger has been found faithful! (2 Timothy 4:1-5; Colossians 1:28-29).

The prophet Hosea described the LORD'S relationship to Israel in covenant terms as one of courtship and betrothal. How deep that goes! His promise to her of His faithfulness is irreversible (Hosea 2:14-20). In that covenant, though, the pledged faithfulness is not one-sided, and neither is it optional. Just like the marriage relationship, both parties are expected to respond to each other in mutual love and faithfulness. In that way, the two become one and reflect one another. As their marriage relationship becomes more solidly established in their abiding love and trust of each other, it becomes immovable and unshakeable. This messenger is in such a state of faithfulness through his continued abiding in his exalted Messiah. His deep love for Him then overflows in his obedience.

The man who through faith is just and upright shall live and shall live by faith. Romans 1:17 AMP Within the words, *shall live*, is the picture of a tree firmly planted by a river: flourishing, giving shade, and producing fruit that remains. James, a half-brother of Jesus, depicts this beautiful dance between faith and obedience when he wrote in his letter about faith's exercise:

> *But, do you desire to come to know, O senseless man! that the aforementioned faith [that exists] apart from works is unproductive? Was not Abraham vindicated by works [justified as to his claim to a living faith] in that he offered his son Isaac on the altar of sacrifice? You see that the aforementioned faith was cooperating and working with his works [and thereby was responsible for their production], and by his works was this faith brought to completion in a well rounded whole. And the scripture was actually and fully realized [brought into operation] which said, 'And Abraham believed God, and it [his act of faith] was put to his account for righteousness. And a friend of God he was called.* James 2:20-23 Wuest

The glorified Christ calls this messenger His friend.

It's important to remember here that true biblical faith is a confident reliance upon God and not solely a mental assent. It's a heart issue that presupposes a revelation from God by the Holy Spirit through His Word. Biblical faith has components: 1) a trust in God that remains steadfast in who He is and that His ways are right, 2) a personal surrender and an allegiance to that truth through His eternal Son Jesus Christ, and 3) and a steadfastness in heart and walk that desires to follow His Son in His ways. Paul helps us to remember this in his letter to the saints at Rome. There we see that Abraham's faith actually rested first in God Himself, not in His promise to him. And like Enoch, his predecessor, His promise to him then became the occasion for the exercise of his faith: *for he who comes to God must believe that He is and that He is a rewarder of those who seek Him.* Hebrews 11:6 Jesus asked Nathaniel a question when He called him to be His disciple. He hasn't stopped asking that same question of those who also want to follow Him: *Do you believe?* (John 1:50).

Because you have kept the word of My perseverance—having entered into the fellowship of His sufferings, this messenger's heart is fully engaged with His. From a humble heart, his burning desire is to be in fellowship with his Lord by listening to His voice and obeying His commandments. To *keep* means to watch with the eye upon and so to guard. It is much like a sentry who stands at attention in order to guard against loss or injury, or to detain in custody if need be. To keep the Lord's word means to keep an eye upon His discourses, teachings, and instructions in order to obey Him. Like a sentry again, it involves fulfilling his duty. With his gaze fixed upon the Lord Jesus, this messenger is faithfully and vigilantly performing the works He requires of His disciples even in the most difficult of afflictions. That is what *the word of My perseverance* means.

To persevere means to remain under or to bear up under. It involves endurance, patience, and constancy under the most severe suffering in both faith and duty. True love is what motivates and energizes perseverance. It is an exercise in spirit and involves a strength in character which does not allow someone to surrender or succumb to pressures of any kind. And for a reason. *Therefore, brethren, be all the more diligent to make certain about His calling and choosing you; for as long as you practice these things, you will never stumble; for in this way the entrance into the eternal kingdom of our Lord and Savior will be abundantly supplied to you.* 2 Peter 1:11

...and have not denied My name (vs. 8). Three young Hebrew men in the days of King Nebuchadnezzar gave a striking witness to their allegiance to the only true God when they refused to bow down and worship the gold image he had set up in the plain of Dura. In a fit of rage, Nebuchadnezzar threatened them with certain death in a burning fiery furnace for their noncompliance. They still stood their ground; they stood true to the God of heaven without hesitating. You see, they truly understood the seriousness of sin itself and that God's holy displeasure against their disobedience would have far worse consequences for them than the wrath they were presently encountering from a mere human being. These three young men did not want to forfeit their lives by bowing down to his image instead of God Himself! In light of that, they then said to King Nebuchadnezzar with hearts full of faith in complete trust and utter loyalty to the living God, *But if not*. With those words, these young men were giving evidence to a true faith that trusts in God and obeys Him regardless of any of its consequences to them. They knew their God (Deuteronomy 32:1-4). Just like them, this messenger also

knows his God. His trust in Him, the One who raises the dead, hasn't wavered. He has persevered and refused to back down from the Lord's name and the essential nature of His Person, even when it meant disappointment, suffering, trouble, persecution, and personal loss to him. Through his absolute dependence upon, adherence to, and trust in his resurrected Christ, he has refused to compromise the integrity of his faith in Him: he has not shied away from, rejected, or disowned Him through his words and actions. And just like the three young Hebrew men, it was this messenger's life of faith in Jesus Christ in the midst of his suffering and persecution that constituted and gave evidence of his faith…not the experience of personal deliverance from it.

At this juncture, one might wonder why. Why would this messenger be willing to be a partaker of the sufferings of Christ at such cost? Like God's friend Abraham, he too had his eyes and affections set on a much higher and far greater glory (Hebrew 11:13-18 Colossians 3:1-4). Having set his mind like a compass point on that reality, he was able to stay the course in the midst of any unbearable circumstances knowing that his human strength wouldn't accomplish anything of eternal value. By having fully submitted himself at each juncture to God's righteousness in Christ, this messenger intentionally and purposefully remained under the Holy Spirit's leadership in him. And like the apostle Paul, when he was burdened beyond his own human strength even to the point of despairing of life itself, he too learned another very valuable lesson in the life of faith. Jesus said to Paul, *My grace is sufficient for you, for power is perfected in weakness. Most gladly, therefore, I will rather boast about my weaknesses, so that the power of Christ may dwell in me. Therefore I am well content with weaknesses, with insults, with distresses, with persecutions, with difficulties, for Christ's sake: for when I am weak, then I am strong.* 2 Corinthians 12:9-10

And in your patience possess ye your souls. Luke 21:19 KJV The Church is on a journey of faith in which she is to blossom forth into full spiritual maturity. The fullness of Christ Himself resides within her, where He is her all and all. An earthen vessel, His Bride especially comes to realize her full potential in Him when persevering in faith in the midst of tears, perplexities, fears, weaknesses, and buffetings. As her gaze remains focused on the Holy One, He who is true and holy, she engages in true devotion through time spent in communion with Him and in reflection on His word, in prayer and in daily (and sometimes moment by moment) resistance to sin, and in fellowship with other believers in a local church. Christ Himself can then manifest His glory within her and around her for all to see! For in His hands, suffering when properly submitted to is a transforming tool that opens her up to the abundance of His grace and allows His life and the stature of His fullness to flow through her to others. For in God's wisdom, victory for a Christian is not necessarily the removal of weakness, nor is it simply the manifestation of His divine power. Victory for a Christian is oftentimes the manifestation of His divine power through human weakness!

> *Now to Him who is able to keep you from stumbling, and to make you stand in the presence of His glory blameless with great joy, to the only God our Savior, through Jesus Christ our Lord, be glory, majesty, dominion and authority, before all time and now and forever.* Jude 24

This messenger certainly understood this. He knew where true strength lies, what it is, and what it accomplishes! (2 Corinthians 4:7-12; John 14:12-13).

CHAPTER SEVEN:
Behold the Cliff

> **To the angel of the church of the Laodiceans write:**
> *The Amen, the faithful and true Witness, the Beginning of the creation of God says this: "I know your deeds, that you are neither cold nor hot. So because you are lukewarm, and neither cold nor hot, I will spit (lit. vomit) you out of My mouth. Because you say, "I am rich, and have become wealthy, and have need of nothing," and you do not know that you are wretched and miserable and poor and blind and naked, I advise you to buy from Me gold refined by fire so that you may become rich, and white garments so that you may clothe yourself, and that the shame of your nakedness will not be revealed; and eye salve to anoint your eye so that you may see. Those whom I love, I reprove and discipline; therefore be zealous and repent. Behold, I stand at the door and knock; if anyone opens the door, I will come in to him and will dine with him and he with Me. He who overcomes, I will grant to him to sit down with Me on My throne, as I also overcame and sat down with My Father on His throne. He who has an ear, let him hear what the Spirit says to the churches.* **Revelation 3:14-22**

In the strategic layout of the seven messages to the seven messengers of the seven churches in Asia, this is the last one. As such, it is considered to be the closest to the Lord's return! So it becomes even more serious and somber when you realize it describes the spiritual condition of worldliness and its idolatry and the apostasy that will be prevalent among the Church's pastoral and apostolic leadership and in their congregations at large as we come into the end of the age of grace. That is why this church in the KJV is addressed as the church of the Laodiceans rather than as the church in Laodicea.

The church of the Laodiceans lived in the midst of a city that was well-known for its wealth and self-sufficiency. Laodicea lay at a very important crossroad of commercial routes and therefore prospered and thrived as a commercial center. In fact, its inhabitants had become so wealthy that they were able to rebuild their city from their own resources and wealth after a devastating earthquake leveled it. Yet in spite of all their ingenuity and apparent successes, the city actually lacked a sufficient and permanent supply of good water!

With this as His backdrop, the Lord Jesus amazingly speaks to the messenger of the church of the Laodiceans in all his failures and spiritual breakdowns as *The Amen, the faithful and true Witness, the Beginning of the creation of God.* The Amen, the beginning of God's creation, is the heavenly Father's Witness to His righteousness. Shortly before His trial, Jesus gave witness to the high priest Caiaphas when pressed by him to answer the question as to whether He was the Christ, the Son of God. He testified: *You have said it yourself; nevertheless I tell you, hereafter you will see THE SON OF MAN SITTING AT THE RIGHT HAND OF POWER, AND COMING ON THE CLOUDS OF HEAVEN.* Matthew 26:64 Jesus gave witness again when Pilate asked Him during His trial if he were a king. He testified, *You say correctly that I am a king. For this I have been born, and for this I have come into the world, to testify to the truth. Everyone who is of the truth hears My voice.* John 18:37.

What direction of life the Lord is pointing this messenger to! The faithful and true Witness sees this messenger's works: he is neither cold—someone who can give a cup of refreshing water to a thirsty soul; nor hot—someone who is zealous for the Lord and going about doing His Father's works. His use of the word *lukewarm* brings about more light on the matter at hand. Water from a faucet that is either cold or hot is always useful to its owner and beneficial toward those who come to it. For cold water is refreshing to the thirsty, while hot water is soothing and relaxing to those who are tense or ill at ease. On the other hand, tepid water from that same faucet is really of very little use, except perhaps for inducing vomiting. With these words, the faithful and true Witness is expressing the intensity of His holy frustration and displeasure with this messenger's seriously backslidden condition. His lukewarmness—his non-productivity as His own offspring and as a spiritual leader within His church—is nauseating Him to the point of spewing him out of His mouth.

This messenger's claim that he is rich, having become increased with goods and is therefore in need of nothing, is a witness to the foolishness of his own pride and unfaithfulness. And more than that, his testimony points to the state of failure and spiritual bankruptcy that he is actually in. Living independently of his God, he has carelessly turned from Him to the world as his reference point and source of fulfillment, much like Solomon did. In a state of coveting and self-indulgence and its various self-inflations, this messenger is destitute of anything of meaningful and eternal value (2 Corinthians 10:17-18; Psalm 49:16-20).

Jesus also said to His disciples,

Chapter Seven: Behold the Cliff

A disciple is not above his teacher, now a slave above his master. It is enough for the disciple that he become like his teacher, and the slave like his master. Matthew 10:24-25a

If anyone wishes to come after Me, he must deny himself, and take up his cross and follow Me. For whoever wishes to save his life will lose it; but whoever loses his life for My sake will find it. For what will it profit a man if he gains the whole world and forfeits his soul? Or what will a man give in exchange for his soul? For the Son of Man is going to come in the glory of His Father with His angels, and will then repay every man according to his deeds. Matthew 16:24-27

What blindness of heart pride breeds! This messenger cannot see he is naked! Having fallen into a lifestyle of feeding his fleshly appetites, his soul is lacking transformation and has been left unclothed. Blind to his own condition, he is living like a beggar on earth instead of a son of God with a glorious high calling and a heavenly inheritance that is his. Like the blind beggar who, at the Lord's command, immediately made his way to the pool of Siloam (which means *sent*) and washed his eyes in those waters, he would do well to do the same. He has to thoroughly wash his spiritually blind eyes in God's Word so he can see as he should and fulfill his calling as both a watchman on the wall and as a true shepherd of His sheep (Ezekiel 33:7-9; 34:1-6).

This is a good place to stop and ask what happened to bring this messenger into such a state of self-indulgence and near apostasy. It began with a subtle lie, as it always does, and one he either failed to recognize or simply ignored and surrendered to without questioning it (James 1:13-17). Having erroneously equated prosperity and success in life with money and material possessions, he then pursued the promises it makes to those who are foolish enough to believe them. Rather than being content with the presence of his exalted Christ within him, he turned back instead to the weak and worthless things of what the world had to offer him. Ensnared now in the trap of measuring success by the world's standard rather than by God's, he has become so engrossed in its false promises that he is missing the mark of God's glorious and larger intention for him and His sons. What a wretched condition indeed! Like the rich man who reasoned within himself about how to hold onto all of his grain and his goods by tearing down his barns and building larger ones, this messenger is living a life of grasping and holding onto things rather than of sharing and sacrificially yielding up his self-life to death. Having increased in material goods, he has sadly believed the lie of self-importance and that he is secure and in need of nothing. But like the reality of any vehicle without gas, the messenger of the church of the Laodiceans is on empty. In fact, without him realizing it, the Lord's glory has departed from him and the congregation! (Luke 12: 15-21;1 Samuel 4:19-22).

That is only the tip of the iceberg. There is a much deeper and far more serious and insidious issue at hand. The pride of his self-assertions is reminiscent of Satan's own five self-assertions of *"I will"* in heaven and its glory (Isaiah 14:12-15). Through that same kind of unchecked pride and self-elevation, this messenger has fallen in league with Satan, doing his bidding in the church and, through it, back out into the world. Instead of eating from the Lord's table as he ought, he has, in fact, been eating at the table of demons. You might well be aghast at that and wondering how that happened.

Through many repeated compromises, both small and big, he has set aside God's grace so he could live out his own life. This messenger's heart is so indifferent and shut off to His Lord now that he is dangerously close to being like Isaac's firstborn son Esau. Through a careless attitude regarding his own birthright, Esau sold it contemptuously to his younger brother Jacob for a mere plate of food. And even though Esau regretted doing that later on, and then sought for that blessing with tears, no place was found in his heart for a true repentance of godly sorrow toward God. This messenger is at a cross point. He must choose now which life he will live. Will it be his self-life or the higher one of everlasting life in Christ and the self-sacrifice that comes with it. *For you were called to freedom, brethren; only do not turn your freedom into an opportunity for the flesh, but through love serve one another.* Galatians 5:13 (1 Corinthians 10:19-22; Luke 6:24-26; 1 Peter 2:16-17).

Proverbs 16:19 also instructs us with these words: *Better it is to be of a humble spirit than to divide the spoil with the proud.* For the reality of true life has always been Christ Jesus Himself, and the full freedom of life in Him is to love your neighbor. To a rich young ruler, Jesus *had these words to say:*

> *If you wish to be complete, go and sell your possessions and give to the poor, and you will have treasure in heaven; and come, follow Me. He who loves his life loses it, and he who hates his life in this world will keep it to eternal life. If anyone serves Me, he must follow Me; and where I am, there My servant will be also; if anyone serves Me, the Father will honor him.* Matthew 19:21; John 12:25-26

The question often arises at this point as to whether the messenger or the members of this church are true believers, given the seriousness and the depth of his and their backsliding. The answer to that question is discovered in verse 19…*Those whom I love, I reprove and discipline; therefore be zealous and repent.* The love mentioned here is that of a parent who carefully brings a child to mature adulthood through guidance, correction, training, and rebuke. Thus, the Amen is speaking here to His own children, not to sinners. Sadly, not having been paid attention to and welcomed by this messenger, He must now stand at the door of His own church and knock, waiting for anyone to open the door so He can come in to them. That knocking there is an admonition and an invitation as well:

> *Do not be bound together with unbelievers; for what partnership have righteousness and lawlessness, or what fellowship has light with darkness? Or what harmony has Christ with Belial, or what has a believer in common with an unbeliever? Or what agreement has the temple of God with idols? For we are the temple of the living God, just as God has said.* 2 Corinthians 6: 14-16a

The answer to Paul's five questions there is *none*. God's answer is, *Therefore, COME OUT FROM THEIR MIDST AND BE SEPARATE, says the Lord. AND DO NOT TOUCH WHAT IS UNCLEAN, AND I WILL WELCOME YOU* (2 Corinthians 6:17).

The Lord's word always comes to us with such direct and precise impact when it's empowered by His Spirit, doesn't it? Notice in His letter to the messenger that the faithful and true

Witness' call is not just to him, but to the church itself! Through his leadership, or should I say, lack of it…the church of the Laodiceans had failed to separate itself or had so appropriated its surrounding culture into the life of the church that there is little if any distinction between it and them. Insipid now, His call is to *anyone* who can hear His voice and respond accordingly. That in itself is a very strong rebuke for this messenger: it's an indication of just how hardened and resistant to the things of God his heart, and many of those in his congregation, had become!

Yet again, another deeper issue is at hand. The word *anyone* is an inclusive word. What a church is morally responsible to God for does not lie solely with its pastoral/apostolic leader. This messenger's responsibility to have watched over and protected and fed His people with proper food does not in and of itself relieve its members from knowing the Truth for themselves or of their responsibility to say something when they know in their spirit that he's off course. In light of that, it's been both the cumulative effects of this messenger's sins as well as that of the congregation's sin of negligence and apathy that has brought about its near apostate condition. Sadly, both have overlooked and forgotten Jesus' question to His disciples in Luke 18:8. *However, when the Son of Man comes, will He find faith (lit. the faith) on the earth?*

Amazingly, a precious promise is given here to *anyone* who hears His voice and opens the door to Him. The Amen says, *I will come in to him and will dine with him, and he with Me.* In the KJV, the word *dine* reads *sup*, meaning *to banquet*. For the Jews, Greeks, and Romans of this era, a banquet was the chief meal taken at or toward evening and often prolonged into the night. Once again, there is a bridal thought here: it is alluding to the marriage supper of the Lamb! When you *sup* with someone, you sit across from each other face to face. This position speaks of both nearness to and personal intimacy with the other person. The Lord's promise is that if *anyone* hears His voice and turns from their sin and begins in a fresh way to seek His face, they will receive HIM in larger and fuller revelations. In this place of the closest intimacy, the Son is privy to all the secret thoughts and desires of His beloved; and His beloved is privy to all of His. It is much like having on a new pair of glasses. Here each child of God, looking beyond themselves to Jesus alone through the Scriptures and the illuminating ministry of the Holy Spirit, will see new dimensions in the life of Christ opening up before them: vistas in eternity their spiritual eyes had not seen before—things planned long ago in eternity are now coming into clearer focus for them as a present-day reality. Those things are not out of their reach after all! For their Father's good pleasure has always been that they enter into the reality of the good news of the glory of Christ and His kingdom whether here on earth or in heaven (John 10:9; 14:8-21; Ephesians 4:11-13; 1 John 3:2-3).

There is much wisdom for whenever He chastens and disciplines those whom He loves. When responded to correctly, it brings about a personal transformation through the rigorous training of righteousness and holiness. For without holiness, it is impossible to see Him. And without seeing Him, little, if anything, can be done that has eternal value and, in this way, falls short of His glory. With each such revelation as they continue on to maturity in Him, they will indeed be ready for His soon return! The faithful and true Witness who cannot lie has said on a number of occasions that He will return for His Bride. His return will be sudden, meaning at any time, and with such swiftness and velocity, there will be no time for any kind of true repentance for anyone not alert and ready for it. He will come that quickly!

Chapter Seven: Behold the Cliff

> *Be dressed in readiness, and keep your lamps lit. Be like men who are waiting for their master when he returns from the wedding feast, so that they may immediately open the door to him when he comes and knocks.* Luke 12:35-36

The banquet table has been set, and the Amen, being the faithful and true Witness that He is, stands at the door of a lukewarm church and knocks. Being the Beginning of God's creation, there is an urgency in His knocking: time is running out!

This messenger is standing on the very brink of a spiritual cliff…one more step in this direction and he surely will topple headlong down its sides to the bottom. It would do him well, and anyone within his congregation who hears that knock, to make an immediate about-face to Him (Isaiah 55:6-8).

Then I turned to see the voice that was speaking to me. And having turned I saw seven golden lampstands; and in the middle of the lampstands I saw one like a son of man, clothed in a robe reaching to the feet, and girded across His chest with a golden sash…As for the mystery of the seven starts which you saw in My right hand, and the seven golden lampstands: the seven stars are the seven angels of the seven churches, and the seven lampstands are the seven churches. Revelation 1:12-13, 20

CHAPTER EIGHT:
A Trumpet Call

Lift up your heads, O gates, and lift them up, O ancient doors, that the King of glory may come in!
Psalm 24:9

The seven messages you have read, along with their specific implications, is an emergency alert to the Church, both to its leadership and the sheep at large. The Lord Jesus is on the very verge of His promised return, yet five leaders and their churches are not alert and prepared, and two are! That is to be taken soberly and is a very serious state of affairs. The very pointedness and brevity of each of these seven messages is the Holy Spirit's eloquent witness in time and eternity of the present-day reality of their risen and exalted Christ being enthroned in heaven… Jesus Christ their Mediator, this Man in glory is coming again just as He has said! (John 14:1-3; Revelation 22:12).

> *The One who holds the seven stars in His right hand, the One who walks among the seven golden lamp stands,*
>
> *The first and the last, who was dead, and has come to life,*
>
> *The One who has the sharp two-edged sword,*
>
> *The Son of God, who has eyes like a flame of fire, and His feet are like burnished bronze,*
>
> *He who has the seven Spirits of God and the seven stars,*

> *He who is holy, who is true, who has the key of David, who opens and no one will shut, and who shuts and no one opens,*
>
> *The Amen, the faithful and true Witness, the Beginning of the creation of God.* Revelation 1:14-16

When the Holy Spirit opens our eyes to the glory of the glorified Christ, it transcends the smallness of our own natural thinking and lifts us up in spirit to see Him in the heights of His infinite and unfathomable majesty as the King of glory. For whenever the Son of God is seen in His glory, the heart is simultaneously humbled and strengthened. Being the great Shepherd of the sheep that He is, He can see beyond the externals to the real need of each messenger and the churches.

Listen carefully now and reflect for a moment on the words of Anne Graham Lotz from her book *The Vision of His Glory.*

> "Pilate, the Roman governor who presided over the trial of Jesus, challenged the rioting mob that shouted for His crucifixion with these words: 'Behold the man!'
>
> That same challenge has been heard down through the centuries: 'Behold the Man!' But the vision the mob beheld has changed from that of a bloodied, tortured, mangled prisoner on His way to execution to a vision of the same Man bathed in glory! The crown of thorns has become a dazzling, bejeweled crown of gold…the seamless robe gambled for by His executioners has become a robe of light, flashing like lightning in its brilliance…

> the hands that were bound now hold the book by which every person who has ever lived will be judged.
>
> The crowds gathered in the courtyard of the judgment hall early that Friday morning, jeering, "Crucify Him! Crucify Him!" give way to multitudes of thousands upon ten thousand who fill the universe with shouts of praise to the One Who alone is worthy of all honor and glory and wisdom and power and strength!
>
> The vision has caused the martyr in the flames of death to smile. It has given strength to the weak, faith to the doubting, courage to the timid, peace to the fearful, victory to the defeated, and hope to the hopeless!
>
> Behold the Man! The vision is glorious!" (Lotz, 1996, 1997, p. xv-xvi).

With each revelation of this Man in glory, there are lessons to be learned by every true servant and witness of His: lessons of their entire dependence upon Him in the moment and for what lies ahead of them in the days to come; and lessons of His sufficiency to meet their need in all the details of their life and service to Him as faithful stewards in His Kingdom. And like John on the island of Patmos who saw the Man of glory and fell down like a dead man at His feet, lessons to remember that it is in the place of such weakness and surrender that His strength and glory can be made known to the world: He, the exalted Christ, is now being seen in them!

Such purposeful and rigorous training and strengthening and empowering of the elect on earth is intended for sacrificial and fruitful living. As they persevere in faith, it is equipping and enabling them to overcome their fleshly appetites and behavior patterns as well as any of Satan's wiles and assaults. With each adjustment and step of faith made by them by the Holy Spirit's power within them, they are becoming stronger in their Lord and the power of His might. Looking away unto Jesus, the author and finisher of their faith, they can stand more firmly now in the faith while ministering in His Name regardless of what it may cost them (Ephesians 6:10-17). For God had no intention of disowning any of the five messengers who received reproof in these two chapters, as some might think or say. A covenant-keeping God, He has all His promises before Him for all His children! (Jeremiah 31:19-20).

The Lord's use of the word *overcomes* in His seven messages is a military word and implies combat with an enemy. *Overcome* means to be victorious, to prevail…in other words, to be more than a conqueror. It is especially indicative here of combat with any of the adversaries of His kingdom and the forces of Satan. His use of the word is a call to spiritual arms for the Church. All believers in Christ are overcomers. That is indeed true (1 John 4:4; 5:4-5). And yet Jesus brought more light to the word when a woman in the crowd exclaimed how blessed His mother was in having Him as her son. He responded and said, *Yea, rather, blessed are they that hear the word of God, and keep it.* Luke 11:27-28 KJV And so too the overcomer who is overcoming; they will emerge in time from the heat and stress of the battle against their own flesh and the wiles of Satan undiscouraged in their faith and undeterred in their vow to live obediently to their God. For Jesus who endured the shame of the Cross did so in order that His Bride, the Church, might also reign with Him both in time and eternity.

Chapter Eight: A Trumpet Call

In each of the seven messages are challenges, and ones to come, that are to be overcome by both the pastoral/apostolic leader and the members of the churches so they can indeed enter into and partake of the promises given to overcomers…not just in the heavenly future that awaits them, but also in their present walks here on earth! Interestingly, the Hebrew word for *overcome* also means to be pure. These are challenges, then, in which they are to adhere more closely to God's standard of Christ-like leadership and holy living found in the Bible by living it out, as well the challenges of a deeper commitment to Christ Jesus up until death or His return, whichever comes first. He, the Alpha and the Omega, has their future in mind for them: *Let us rejoice and be glad and give the glory to Him, for the marriage of the Lamb has come and His Bride has made herself ready.* Revelation 19:7 Such training in holiness and righteousness is equipping and preparing them for that Day! And as that Day is quickly approaching, intense worldwide persecution and pressures will increasingly surround and come up against the Church for her strong stance in her Lord Jesus Christ. Overcomers in Him who are overcoming must continue to hold fast to the Truth and the gospel of the Kingdom at all costs, steadfastly refuting and squelching any doctrinal errors that make their bid to come in, in addition to any of the world's philosophies and wisdom, any of their branding and marketing appeals with their glitz and glamour, any of their standards of thinking and living, and any of their ungodly values and immorality.

The Lord's byword for all overcomers is *hold fast.* That means to take hold of or grasp and not let go. It also means to have power over, to be dominant, or become master of. *Holding fast* implies here a certain degree of force; the kind of force with which someone brings a person or thing wholly under their power even when strong resistance is encountered. It's like sailing a ship with the wind in its sails, holding it toward its point of destination until reached. It also means to be strong, to be mighty, to prevail. Like Jacob, with whom a Man wrestled earnestly throughout the night, refusing to let go of Him unless He blessed him. Jacob had an encounter here with the living God that so changed his perspective and way of thinking that He changed his name accordingly. *He said, Your name shall no longer be Jacob, but Israel (lit. Prince of God): for you have striven with God and with men and have prevailed.* Genesis 32:28

Jacob named that place Peniel: the face of God. There is also Stephen, the first martyr of the Church. While holding fast to his testimony of the Lord Jesus Christ and staring death in the face, he gazed intently into heaven and saw God's glory and Jesus Himself, the Son of Man, standing there at His Father's right hand. Moments later, while being stoned to death for giving his testimony of both them and Him, Stephen held fast and called upon Him who is able to deliver from death saying, *Lord, Jesus, receive my spirit! Then falling on his knees, he cried out with a loud voice, Lord, do not hold this sin against them! Having said this, he fell asleep.* Acts 7:59-60 And just like his Lord, Stephen's life wasn't taken from him but rather given to the enthroned Christ out of deep sacrificial love.

Within these two chapters of Revelation, you see not only specific commendations and corrections given to specific messengers and their churches, but specific promises that come along with them. These promises are for every true believer in Christ. They are from God the Father and are spoken to them by His Son, the faithful and true Witness. These promises become even more amazing when you realize that in His mind, they have within them both a present and future reward for overcomers who overcome a specific challenge. How encouraging and strengthening that is for us. There is hope indeed! Like stepping stones, they are the very ground and strength for a deeper walk with His Son in this life and its reward now, as well as for their richer fulfillment in the heavenly life to come. Whether in baby steps or in the steps of the more mature, or somewhere in between, every act of courage and faith and love will be blessed according to His promises here. Again, all that the Amen has promised to be and do for His Bride, His covenant people, He is doing in the now and will do in the future. What an encouragement for us to persevere in spirit and in faith. And as each believer overcomes, they collectively give proof to their living faith in their living Christ! The overcomers' part in the equation is to simply believe...to act on what they have heard (1 Timothy 4:7-8; 2 Peter 1:2-4; Hebrews 6:13-15).

> *...Christ also loved the church and gave Himself up for her, so that He might sanctify her, having cleansed her by the washing of water with the word, that He might present to Himself the church in all her glory, having no spot or wrinkle or any such thing; but that she would be holy and blameless.* Ephesians 5:25b-27

Surely one of the most profound truths in all Holy Scripture is that the Father always intended to reveal His glory in the face of His Son to the elect out into the world...much like the sun that shines in its strength. The Church, both by her design and establishment, is to give Light into this dark world. For God the Father never intended His Son's Bride to be without the presence and power of His Spirit and the supernatural. In the house of the great King, there is indeed power for miracles that set captives free and heal the brokenhearted. Therein the Holy Spirit works to bring His children into deeper works within them—places in their souls where there is a greater need of sanctification and purification and of being conformed into His Son's image. Here the Lord Jesus increases, and they decrease as they yield—giving the right of way to the Holy Spirit and His Lordship and the work of the Cross in them. For the pathway to life in God's mind has always been through the Cross: here where the self-life is dealt with and His only begotten Son rises in His resurrection glory and is seen. Oh, such glory! Think for a moment of the power that is released when an atom is broken. How much more than when one of His children is! (Philippians 3:7-11; Acts 4:29-30; Galatians 3:5).

> *My Father is glorified by this, that you bear much fruit, and so prove to be My disciples.* John 15:8

As a fruitful vine by a spring whose branches run over a wall, the Church must remain undaunted in her abiding and exalted position in the heavenly places with Christ as she advances His Kingdom here on earth until His return. Here she cleaves to her Bridegroom, holding fast to Him as her crucified, risen, ascended, and exalted King! And that cleaving is where she can enter more freely and fully into Him and the Spirit's work of establishing His Kingdom in her heart and out into the earth. By taking hold of the glorified and exalted Christ in faith and abiding by all that implies, by accepting God's standard of holy living as revealed in His Word and holding fast to His teachings, by remaining in community and fellowship with other believers in a local church, and by laying hold of the hope that has been set before her with joyful anticipation and deep longing for her Bridegroom's promised return, she will remain faithful to Him in her words and deeds as she rises up and reflects Him in the earth during His absence and until He returns (Genesis 48:22-26).

> *But in those days, after that tribulation, THE SUN WILL BE DARKENED AND THE MOON WILL NOT GIVE ITS LIGHT AND THE STARS WILL BE FALLING from heaven, and the powers that are in the heavens will be shaken. Then they will see THE SON OF MAN COMING IN CLOUDS with great power and glory. And then He will send forth the angels, and will gather together His elect from the four winds, from the farthest end of the earth to the farthest end of heaven.*
>
> *Now learn the parable from the fig tree: when its branch has already become tender and puts forth its leaves, you know that summer is near. Even so, you too, when you see these things happening, recognize that He is near, right at the door. Truly I say to you, this generation will not pass away until all these take place. Heaven and earth will pass away, but My words will not pass away. But of that day or hour no one knows, not even the angels in heaven, nor the Son, but the Father alone.*
>
> *Take heed, keep on the alert; for you do not know when the appointed time will come. It is like a man away on a journey, who upon leaving his house and putting his slaves in charge, assigning to each one his task, also commanded the doorkeeper to stay on the alert. Therefore, be on the alert—for you do not know when the master of the house is coming, whether in the evening, at midnight, or when the rooster crows, or in the morning—in case he should come*

> *suddenly and find you asleep. What I say to you, I say to all. Be on the alert.* Mark 13:24-37

He who has an ear, let him hear what the Spirit has said to the churches.

Father, I repent now of my casualness and even indifference towards Your Son's second coming. The lamp of my heart is not aglow as it should be with that deep desire and its joyful anticipation for His promised return. My affections get caught up instead in the trappings of the daily living of life. I do not wake up in the morning thinking, "Will this be the day?" I often think about the joy of entering heaven and seeing Your Son face to face for the first time, but I can't honestly say that I live my day out with the eyes of my heart looking for His return on those clouds of glory. My eyes have been set on instead on lesser things, the mundane and ordinary things of earthly living. I am so very sorry for this. Please accept this genuine repentance and my confession of sin. And please create in my heart that deep desire with its joyful anticipation along with a daily awareness of my Bridegroom's imminent return. Work in me that which is well-pleasing to you, Father…a life laid down for the glory of Your Son's name, and if need be, to die for Him.

Let the Church now say, "Amen."

CHAPTER NINE:
A Deeper Reflection in Truth

> *Then I heard something like the voice of a great multitude and like the sound of many waters and like the sound of mighty peals of thunder, saying, "Hallelujah! For the Lord our God, the Almighty, reigns. Let us rejoice and be glad and give the glory to Him, for the marriage of the Lamb has come and His bride has made herself ready.* Revelation 19:6-7

And behold, I am coming speedily. Blessed (happy and to be envied) is he who observes and lays to heart and keeps the truths of the prophecy—the predictions, consolations and warnings—contained in this little book. Revelation 22:7 AMP

For the Lord Himself will descend from heaven with a shout, with the voice of the archangel and with the trumpet of God, and the dead in Christ will rise first. Then we who are alive and (who) remain will be caught up together with them in the clouds to meet the Lord in the clouds, and so we shall always be with the Lord. 1 Thessalonians 4:16-17

For this reason we must pay much closer attention to what we have heard, so that we do not drift away from it. For if the word spoken through angels proved unalterable, and every transgression and disobedience received a just penalty, how will we escape if we neglect so great a salvation? Hebrews 2:1-3

See to it that you do not refuse Him who is speaking. For if those who did not escape when they refused him who warned them on earth, much less will we escape who turn away from Him who warns from heaven. Hebrews 12:25

Behold, I am coming like a thief. Blessed is the one who stays awake and keeps his clothes, so that he will not walk about naked and men will see his shame. Revelation 16:15

But if we judged ourselves rightly, we would not be judged. But when we are judged, we are disciplined by the Lord so that we will not be condemned along with the world. 1 Corinthians 11:31-32

Then Jesus said to His disciples, If anyone wishes to come after Me, he must deny himself, and take up his cross and follow Me. For whoever wishes to save his life will lose it; but whoever loses his life for My sake will find it. For what will it profit a man if he gains the whole world and forfeits his soul? Or what will a man give in exchange for his soul. For the Son of Man is going to come in the glory of His Father with His angels, and will then repay every man according to his deeds. Matthew 16:24-27

We are children of God: and if children, then heirs; heirs of God, and joint heirs with Christ; if so be that we suffer with Him, that we may be glorified with Him. For I reckon that the sufferings of this present time are not worthy to be compared with the glory which shall be revealed to usward. Romans 8:16-18 KJV

But let us, who are of the day, be sober; putting on the breastplate of faith and love; and for a helmet, the hope of salvation. For God has not appointed us to wrath, but to obtain salvation by our Lord Jesus Christ, who died for us, that, whether we wake or sleep, we should live together with Him. 1 Thessalonians 5:8-10 KJV

Chapter Nine: A Deeper Reflection in Truth

But have nothing to do with worldly fables fit only for old women. On the other hand, discipline yourself for the purpose of godliness; for bodily discipline is only for a little profit, but godliness is profitable for all things, since it holds promise for the present life and also for the life to come. It is a trustworthy statement deserving full acceptance. For it is for this we labor and strive, because we have fixed our hope on the living God, who is the Savior of all men, especially of believers. 1 Timothy 4:7-10

And in as much as it is appointed for men to die once and after this comes judgment, so Christ also having been offered once to bear the sins of many, will appear a second time for salvation without reference to sin, to those who eagerly await Him. Hebrews 9:27-28

You therefore, beloved, knowing this beforehand, be on your guard so that you are not carried away by the error of unprincipled men and fall from your own steadfastness, but grow in the grace and knowledge of our Lord and Savior Jesus Christ. To Him be the glory, both now and to the day of eternity. Amen. 2 Peter 3:17-18

Therefore, my beloved brethren, be steadfast, immovable, always abounding in the work of the Lord, knowing that your toil is not in vain in the Lord. 1 Corinthians 15:58

CHAPTER TEN:
The Judgment of Believers

From KJV *Life in the Spirit Study Bible*
Published by Zondervan (www.zondervan.com)

Concerning the judgment of believers, the following facts should be kept in mind:

(1) All Christians will be subject to judgment; there will be no exceptions (Rom. 14:12; 1 Cor. 3:12-15; 2 Cor. 5:10; see Eccl. 12:14, note).

(2) This judgment will occur when Christ returns for His Church (see John 14:3, note; 1 Thes. 4:14-17).

(3) The judge is Christ (John 5:22; 2 Tim. 4:8).

(4) The Bible speaks of the believer's judgment as something solemn and serious, especially since it includes the possibility of damage or "loss" (1 Cor. 3:15; 2 John 8), of being ashamed before Him "at His coming" (1 John 2:28) and of burning up one's whole life's work (1 Cor. 3:13-15). The believer's judgment, however, will not involve a declaration of condemnation by God.

(5) Everything will be made manifest. The word *appear* (Gk *phanee*, 2 Cor. 5:10) means "to be revealed openly or publicly." God will examine and openly reveal, in its true reality, (a) our secret acts (Mark 4:22; Rom. 2:16), (b) our character (Rom. 2:5-11), (c) our words (Matt. 12:36-37), (d) our good deeds (Eph. 6:8), (e) our attitudes (Matt. 5:22), (f) our motives (1

Cor. 4:5), (g) our lack of love (Col. 3:18-4:1), and (h) our work and ministry (1 Cor. 3:13).

(6) In sum, believers will have to give an account of their faithfulness or unfaithfulness to God (Matt. 25:21,23; 1 Cor. 4:2-5) and of their deeds in light of the grace, opportunity, and understanding made available to them (Luke 12:48; John 5:24; Rom. 8:1).

(7) The believer's bad deeds, when repented of, are forgiven with respect to eternal punishment (Rom. 8:1), but they are still taken into account when being judged for repayment: *"He that doeth wrong shall receive for the wrong which he hath done"* (Col. 3:25; cf. Eccl. 12:14; 1 Cor. 3:15; 2 Cor. 5:10). The believer's good deeds and love are remembered by God and rewarded (Heb. 6:10): *"Whatsoever good thing any man doeth, the same shall he receive of the Lord"* (Eph. 6:8).

(8) The specific results of the believer's judgment will be varied. There will be either the gain or loss of joy (1 John 2:28), divine approval (Matt. 25:21), tasks, and authority (Matt. 25:14-30), position (Matt. 5:19; 19:30), rewards (1 Cor. 3:12-14; Phil. 3:14; 2 Tim. 4:8), and honor (Rom. 2:10; cf. 1 Pet.1:7).

(9) The impending judgment of Christians should perfect in them the fear of the Lord (2 Co. 5:11; Phil. 2:12; 1 Pet. 1:17) and cause them to be clear-minded and self-controlled, to watch and pray (1 Pet. 4:5,7), to live holy and godly lives (2 Pet. 3:11), and to show mercy and kindness to all (Matt. 5:7; cf. 2 Tim. 1:16).

Chapter Eleven:
The Glorified One

Abide in Christ by Andrew Murray

This classic reprint was previously published under the title Abide in Christ: Thoughts on the Blessed Life of Fellowship with the Son of God in London by James Nisbet & Company in 1888.

Your life is hid with Christ in God. When Christ, who is our life, shall appear, then shall ye also appear with Him in glory.
Colossians 3:3-4 KJV

He that abides in Christ, the Crucified One, learns to know what it is to be crucified with Him, and in Him to be indeed dead unto sin. He that abides in Christ the Risen and Glorified One becomes in the same way partaker of His resurrection life, and of the glory with which He has now been crowned in heaven. Unspeakable are the blessings which flow to the soul from the union with Jesus in His glorified life.

This life is a life of *perfect victory and rest*. Before His death, the Son of God had to suffer and to struggle, could be tempted and troubled by sin and its assaults; as the Risen One, He has triumphed over sin; and as the Glorified One, His humanity has entered into the participation of the glory of Deity. The believer who abides in Him as such is led to see how the power of sin and the flesh are destroyed: the consciousness of complete and everlasting deliverance becomes increasingly clear, and the blessed rest and peace, the fruit of such a conviction that victory and deliverance are an accomplished fact, take possession of the

Chapter Eleven: The Glorified One

life. Abiding in Jesus, in whom he has been raised and set in the heavenly places, he receives of that glorious life streaming from the Head through every member of the body.

This life is a life in *the full fellowship of the Father's love and holiness.* Jesus often gave prominence to this thought with His disciples. His death was a going to the Father. He prayed: "Glorify Me, O Father, *with Thyself,* with the glory which I had *with Thee."* As the believer, abiding in Christ the Glorified One, seeks to realize and experience what His union with Jesus on the throne implies, he apprehends how the unclouded light of the Father's presence is His highest glory and blessedness, and in Him the believer's portion too. He learns the sacred art of always, in fellowship with His exalted head, dwelling in the secret of the Father's presence. Further, when Jesus was on earth, temptation could still reach Him: in glory, everything is holy, and in perfect harmony with the will of God. And so the believer who abides in Him experiences that in this high fellowship, his spirit is sanctified into growing harmony with the Father's will. The heavenly life of Jesus is the power that casts out sin.

This life is a life of *loving beneficence and activity.* Seated on His throne, He dispenses His gifts, bestows His Spirit, and never ceases in love to watch and to work for those who are His. The believer cannot abide in Jesus, the Glorified One, without feeling himself stirred and strengthened to work: the Spirit and the love of Jesus breathe the will and the power to be a blessing to others. Jesus went to heaven with the very object of obtaining power there to bless abundantly. He does this as the heavenly Vine only through the medium of His people as His branches. Whoever, therefore, abides in Him, the Glorified One, bears fruit, for he receives of the Spirit and the power of the eternal life of his exalted Lord, and becomes the channel through which the fullness of Jesus, who hath been exalted to be a Prince and a Savior, flows out to bless those around him.

There is one more thought in regard to this life of the Glorified One, and ours in Him. It is a life of *wondrous expectation and hope*. It is so with Christ. He sits at the right hand of God, *expecting*, till all His enemies be made His footstool, looking forward to the time when He shall receive His full reward, when His glory shall be made manifest, and His beloved people be ever with Him in that glory. The hope of Christ is the hope of His redeemed: "I will come again and take to myself, that where I am there, ye may be also." This promise is as precious to Christ as it ever can be to us. The joy of meeting is surely no less for the coming bridegroom than for the waiting bride. The life of Christ in glory is one of longing expectation: the full glory only comes when His beloved are with Him.

The believer who abides closely in Christ will share with Him in this spirit of expectation. Not so much for the increase of personal happiness, but from the spirit of enthusiastic allegiance to his King, he longs to see Him come in His glory, reigning over every enemy, the full revelation of God's everlasting love. "Till He come" is the watchword of every true-hearted believer. "Christ shall appear, and we shall appear with Him in glory."

There may be very serious differences in the exposition of the promises of His coming. To one, it is plain as day that He is coming very speedily in person to reign on earth, and that speedy coming is his hope and his stay. To another, loving his Bible and his Savior no less, the coming can mean nothing but the judgment day—the solemn transition from time to eternity, the close of history on earth, the beginning of heaven; and the thought of that manifestation of his Savior's glory in no less his joy and his strength. It is Jesus, Jesus coming again, Jesus taking us to Himself, Jesus adored as Lord of all, that is to the whole Church the sum and the center of its hope.

It is by abiding in Christ the Glorified One that the believer will be quickened to that truly spiritual looking for His coming, which alone brings true blessing to the soul. There is an interest in the study of the things which are to be, in which the discipleship of a school is often more marked than the discipleship of Christ the meek; in which contendings for opinions and condemnation of brethren are more striking than any signs of the coming glory. It is only the humility that is willing to learn from those who may have other gifts and deeper revelations of the truth that we, and the love that always speaks gently and tenderly of those who see not as we do, and the heavenliness that shows that the Coming One is indeed already our life, that will persuade either the Church or the world that this our faith is not in the wisdom of men, but in the power of God. To testify of the Savior as the Coming One, we must be abiding in and bearing the image of Him as the Glorified One. Not the correctness of the views we hold, nor the earnestness with which we advocate them, will prepare us for meeting Him, but only the abiding in Him. Then only can our being manifested with Him be what it is meant to be—a transfiguration, a breaking out and shining forth of the indwelling glory that had been waiting for the day of revelation.

Blessed life! "the life hid with Christ in God," "set in the heavenlies in Christ," abiding in Christ the glorified! Once again, the question comes: Can a feeble child of dust really dwell in fellowship with the King of glory? And again, the blessed answer has to be given: To maintain that union is the very work for which Christ has all power in heaven and earth at His disposal. The blessing will be given to him who will trust his

Lord for it, who in faith and confident expectation ceases not to yield himself to be wholly one with Him. It was an act of wondrous though simple faith, in which the soul yielded at first to the Savior. That faith grows up to clearer insight and a faster hold of God's truth that we are one with Him in His glory. In that same wondrous faith, wondrously simple, but wondrously mighty, the soul learns to abandon itself entirely to the keeping of Christ's almighty power and the actings of His eternal life. Because it knows that it has the Spirit of God dwelling within to communicate all that Christ is, it no longer looks upon it as a burden or a work, but allows the divine life to have its way, to do its work; its faith is the increasing abandonment of self, the expectation and acceptance of all that the love and the power of the Glorified One can perform. In that faith, unbroken fellowship is maintained, and growing conformity realized. As with Moses, the fellowship makes partakers of the glory, and the life begins to shine with a brightness not of this world.

Blessed life! *It is* ours, for Jesus is ours. Blessed life! We have the possession within us in its hidden power, and we have the prospect before us in its fullest glory. May our daily lives be the bright and blessed proof that the hidden power dwells within, preparing us for the glory to be revealed. May our abiding in Christ the Glorified One be our power to live to the glory of the Father, our fitness to share in the glory of the Son.

AND NOW,
LITTLE CHILDREN,
ABIDE IN HIM,
THAT, WHEN HE SHALL APPEAR, WE MAY HAVE
CONFIDENCE, AND NOT BE ASHAMED
BEFORE HIM AT HIS COMING.

Chapter Twelve:
A Revived Church

Revival by Andrew Murray
Originally published: Coming Revival. London: Pickering & Inglis, 1989

> *"God be merciful unto us, and bless us; and cause His face to shine on us; that Thy way may be known upon earth, Thy saving health among all nations... God, even our God, shall bless us. God shall bless us; and all the ends of the earth shall fear Him."* Psalm 67:1-2, 6-7 KJV

In speaking of and praying for revival, it is important that we understand what we really desire and ask for. To most Christians, the word conveys the meaning of a large increase in the number of conversions. When that happens, they say, "There has been quite a revival in that church (or town)."

The true meaning of the word is far deeper. The word means making alive again those who have been alive but have fallen into what is called a cold, or dead, state. They are Christians and have life, but they need reviving to bring them back to their first love and the healthy growth of spiritual life, which conversion was meant to be the entrance. When the church as a whole, its ministers and members, is not living in full wholehearted devotion to Christ and His service, is not walking in the joy of the Lord and separation from the world, we need to pray, more than for the conversion of the unconverted, that God's people may truly be revived and the life of God in power restored to them.

It may be said: Is not adding new converts the best way of reviving the church? Does not that awaken interest, and gladness, and the Christians to new activity? This may be true and yet not meet the real need for two reasons: First, such a revival is generally very temporary and soon leaves the church settling down to its ordinary level. Second, these converts, when brought into a church that is not living in the warmth of true spiritual life—in all holiness and fruitfulness—are not helped as they need and do not rise above the lukewarmness around them.

What we need to pray and labor for, first of all, is that the church of true believers may be revived. What the world needs above everything is not mere men and women of the ordinary of Christians but better people. We need Christians who are stronger in faith and holier in life, intensely devoted to Christ and His service and ready to sacrifice all for the salvation of souls. When God's Spirit is poured out upon the church of men and women, who are now struggling on in feebleness, are clothed with the garments of praise and the power of the Holy Spirit, the world will soon share the blessing. These revived believers will be ready to give themselves to God's work at home or abroad; their word and witness will be in power. Nominal Christians will be judged by the power of the revived ones' example and will confess that God is with them. And the world will, in the increased numbers and the burning fervor of the messengers of a quickened church, share in the blessing. A revival among believers is the great need of our day. A revived church is the only hope of a dying world.

Chapter Twelve: A Revived Church

If our conviction of this truth is to be deep and influential, if by it our desire and faith and prayer for revival are really to be stirred and strengthened, we need the Holy Spirit of God to reveal the meaning of such words in the light of God's purpose. The spiritual character of the church, its great object as the instrument of God's almighty power in conquering the world, and the conditions under which that purpose can be accomplished, are all thoughts of God—that God Himself shows what His church is meant to be, what He has promised to be to it, and how His plan with her is to be carried out. Let us try to think out some of the great thoughts of God as revealed in His Word.

The church has the charge of the world entrusted to it. When Christ finished His work on earth and went to heaven to carry it on there, He spoke of two powers to whom the continuation of the work on earth was to be committed to. He spoke of the Holy Spirit, who should come in His name to convict the world and be a divine power in His disciples to reveal Himself in them, and so make them witnesses for Him to the ends of the earth. He spoke of His disciples as those whom He sent into the world, even as the Father sent Him. Just as entirely as He had lived to do the Father's will in saving men and women, so was His Spirit to do that work, too. And just as wholly as the Spirit was to be devoted to that work was the body, the church to be set apart for it. The whole body of believers, and every individual believer, was to be like Christ, the light of the world, placed in the world with one definite, exclusive object of enlightening its darkness and bringing men and women out of darkness into light.

To do its work, the church has the promise of the power of the Holy Spirit of God. That Spirit is given to every believer to be within him the power of a divine and holy life. That Spirit is to be to him the seal of his worship and acceptance, the fountain of love and joy, the grace for conquering sin and the world, the power to do all that God would have us to do. That Spirit is to enlighten and guide and lead, to sanctify and fit for unbroken fellowship with a holy God, to reveal Christ the Son of God the Father within the heart. He is to be a fountain springing up within and flowing forth as streams of living water in what He thus works in personal experience; He equips the person to boldly testify about God's power and to communicate to others what has happened in his own life. Without the power of the Holy Spirit fully recognized and experienced, the church cannot know or fulfill its calling. With His power, the life and fruit God asks for are natural and sure. When the Holy Spirit does not work in power, it is proof that another spirit has been allowed to take its place.

There are only two spirits in the spiritual world—the Spirit of God and the spirit of the world. Between these, there is an unceasing struggle going on. It is because Christians live so much for this present world, and under its power, that its spirit gets possession of them and grieves and quenches the Spirit of God. They lose the power to conquer sin or live a holier life. They lose any intense desire to live for God and His kingdom. They lose the divine love that would enable them to live for or to have an influence on their neighbors. Their religion becomes that of the mind and not for the heart. They are willing to listen to beautiful words on religion and count the pleasing impressions these make as religious feeling. And all the while, they are quenching the life in them into impotence and death. This is the state in which multitudes of Christians live, making themselves and their churches powerless for good or blessing.

It is out of this state that a revival is needed to lift the church into its true life, according to the divine pattern. A true revival

Chapter Twelve: A Revived Church

means nothing less than a revolution, casting out the spirit of worldliness and selfishness and making God and His love triumph in the heart and life. As every birth has its travails and its pangs, so this entrance of a new divine life in power into a church must be preceded and accompanied by the pains of conviction and confession, by the earnest searchings of heart in which sin is discovered, is held up to shame, and condemned. In such a work of grace, many will learn how little truth or power there has been either in their conversion or their spiritual life. They will see things that they tolerated to be vile sin that nothing but the blood of Christ can wash away and the power of Christ can overcome. They will no longer wonder at someone speaking of the need of a second conversion; the experience of many will teach them that the change is even greater. They will see that now, for the first time, they truly know what the power of grace is, what the blessedness of God's love is, and what the joy of a heart given to His service is. And the work of Christ will be the spontaneous fruit of God's Spirit coming on them.

On those who believe that a revival is needed and is possible rests the solemn responsibility of preparing the way of the Lord in speaking to God and men and women about it. To God, we speak about it in prayer. We ask Him to open our own eyes and hearts, and those of our church, to what He thinks and says of the spiritual life He finds. We confess our own sin and the sin of our brethren. We give ourselves to stand in the gap, to take hold of God's strength. We ask the Spirit to give us the consciousness of being intercessors, who in tender love, and yet in holy zeal and truth, speak to God about the state in which His church is. Not in the spirit of judgment or self-exaltation, but in deep humility and the spirit of self-sacrifice, we ask God to show us if it is true what we think we see—that the spirit of self-will and the world is robbing the church of its power to continue to carry out the work Christ began. We ask God to reveal to us if and how deliverance can come.

And so we are prepared to lift up our testimony and speak to our brethren. It may not happen at once: the fire may burn long in our bones. It may not be to large audiences, or with any marked result. But if our speaking to men is the fruit of much speaking to God, of real waiting on Him for revival, it must tell. As one here and another there—this is usually God's way—begins to see what God's will really is concerning His church, the cause of her failure, and the path of restoration and what the certainty of the visitation of His grace, his prayer will become more urgent and believing, and the blessing will come.

All this must lead to the assured faith that a revived church is a possibility, a promise, and a certainty. As in the individual and his needs, so with the church and the mighty change to be wrought in it: unbelief is the great hindrance. And faith can triumph only where it stands, not in the wisdom of men and in the hope they have of revival from all the agencies that are at work, and all the progress they see, but in the power of God and His direct intervention. Faith looks up to and worships the God of absolute omnipotence and infinite love. God can, God will—these are the foundational strengths, on the right hand and on the left.

Yes, God is able! It needs but an act of His will, and His Holy Spirit, the mighty power of God working in His church, can give new life to all who long to receive Him. He can work conviction in those who are resting content in external prosperity and human agencies. He can give the joy of the Holy Spirit, first in single churches and then in larger bodies. He can awaken His people, as out of sleep, to see, consent, and rejoice that they are indeed the hope of a dying world. And God is ready! As the sun pours its light and warmth on every tiny flower to give its growth and beauty, God's love is waiting and longing to pour itself into hearts that reach out after Him. Sometimes it may appear as if He waits long and delays His coming. But let us be sure of this: He does not wait one moment longer than is needful. We may depend on it, with the utmost confidence, that if His children unite in praying for a revived church as the only hope of a dying world, He will hear the prayer.

Let us give ourselves to prayer—intelligent, deliberate, intense prayer. I now venture to offer to God's children what I trust may be a help in praying for revival. I wish to begin by showing what is lacking in the life of the church and the causes to which it is attributed. I then propose to invite my readers to set their hearts on the pattern given in the Sermons on the Mount, according to which everything in the life of the believer and the church ought to be regulated. I shall ask them to pray very specially that God would give them and all god's people a vision of what He expects His church to be, of what He has promised He is able to and actually can make it be. In the light of that vision, may the conviction be deepened of how impossible it is for us to rest satisfied with the present church. This will prepare us for realizing the utter impotence of all human efforts and the necessity of looking up for a divine intervention. It will compel us to listen earnestly to God's Word concerning the almighty power in which He is ready to work. We will see that in our own personal experience, we may prove. And be able to testify confidently to others that God does a new thing in the earth, that He does enable His children to live lives holy and exact obedience, of joyous and complete consecration to His service. We shall then be ready to believe with a new intensity in the

Holy Spirit. For He can fill the hearts of God's saints and clothe them with the power that fits them for conquering the world.

It is hardly necessary to say how varied the elements of prayer suggested by such a study will be. It will begin with heart-searching, confession, and humiliation. The Holy Spirit will show us what part we have had in the universal defection, even while we deplored it. He will judge us in things that have been tolerated. He will open our eyes to see what is wrong around us and to come to God himself bearing the burden of worldliness and self-contentment of His children, who are one body with us.

As we study and see what God has promised, and connect that with the individual churches or the larger bodies to which we belong, we shall feel what a solemn thing it is to offer ourselves as intercessors to God and witnesses with men, in regard to the dishonor done to His name. The word *revival* will get a new meaning and fullness of thought; the prayer for it a new urgency; the effectual prevailing prayer a new demand. As the solemn words "a revived church the only hope for a dying world" are borne in us and burned into us, prayer and intercession will become a transaction with God. Our utter helplessness will have to take hold of and cling to His almighty power. Our whole life must become possessed by the thought that there is nothing worth living for but the will of God in the salvation of men.

REFERENCES

Lotz, Anne Graham (1997). *The Vision of His Glory: Finding Hope Through the Revelation of Jesus Christ.* Word Pub.

Murray, Andrew (1885). *Abide in Christ: Thoughts of the Blessed Life of Fellowship with the Son of God.* London.

Murray, Andrew (1990). *Revival.* Bethany House.

Nee, Watchman (2006). *The Normal Christian Life.* Hendrickson Publishers, Inc.

Spurgeon, C.H. (2008). *Morning and Evening.* Christian Heritage.

Stamps, Donald C, & J Wesley Adams (2003). *Life in the Spirit Study Bible: King James Version.* Zondervan.

Wuest, Kenneth Samuel (1988). *The New Testament: An Expanded Translation.* Grand Rapids, Eerdmans.

The Comparative Study Bible (1984). by the Zondervan Corporation, Grand Rapids

About the Author

Marjorie's salvation came in the early evening hours of December 22, 1984. After having heard the gospel preached for eleven months at Emmanuel Baptist Church in San Jose, California, she humbled herself before God, and by faith in the Lord Jesus Christ, confessed her need to Him for His forgiveness and her salvation. Immediately she knew she was different and forever changed: she had passed from darkness into Light. She then acted on that truth by being water baptized on February 3, 1985.

Hungry to know her Lord more deeply, she enrolled in a three-year course of biblical studies in September of 1987 at Faith Bible College in San Jose. She graduated with an Associate Degree in Biblical Studies on May 24, 1990, and shortly thereafter began evangelizing children in neighborhoods through Bible clubs. Her calling being confirmed by church leadership, she then stepped out in faith according to Matthew 10:10 into full-time ministry in January 1992.

She has been an active member at Abundant Christian Fellowship in Mountain View, California, beginning in December 2009. She serves primarily in the women's ministry and in discipling women, as well as for altar prayer. A gifted teacher in God's Word, Marjorie's passion is to see Christ glorified in His church by believers experiencing a more intimate fellowship with Him through the revelatory ministry of the Holy Spirit, and in this way be built up in their faith. She has also written and published another book entitled *The Voice of The Call of God*.

Notes

Notes

Notes

Notes

Notes

Notes

www.ingramcontent.com/pod-product-compliance
Lightning Source LLC
Chambersburg PA
CBHW050329120526
44592CB00014B/2116